GET THE POWER TO CHANGE YOUR LIFE

TERRY GOGNA
INTERNATIONAL SPEAKER & AUTHOR

Get The Power To Change Your Life

By Terry Gogna

Edited by Anil Gogna and Aaron Gogna

Published by Terry Gogna Inc.
www.TerryGogna.com

ISBN: 9780990791829

Printed in the USA.

B O O K D E S I G N A N D L A Y O U T

Pearl and Everett

www.PearlandEverett.com

Terry Gogna,
Thank you for taking your time and
reading this not proffesional letter.
Whenever you feel you are lying to
yourself with your work, just remeber:
In november 18 of 2012 in Dominican
Republic you impacted hundreds of
lifes, but specially mine. I am simply
a sixteen year old girl inside the business
looking for something worth living for.
I suffer from severe depression, my brother
suicide, I do not have a relationship with
my parents... and thanks to you I know
I simply can not quit. I want to take care
of my grandmother who lives in Ukraine (she
raised me), I want to have a relationship with
God, and most of all I want to be happy.
Thank you for sharing your life with me,
now I know how I want my life to be.

Have a great flight,
hope to see you soon in DR.

To my beautiful parents,
I thank you both,
not just for giving me life,
but more importantly,
for giving me love.

CONTENTS

Introduction

Sometimes when life gets really tough, it's not strength or power that we always need first. Power without peace can become exhausting.

At those unexpected times, when life knocks us down, motivation to do something great with our lives is not always what we want at that very moment. Often, we first just need to feel a sense of peace amongst all the turmoil, stress and tears.

Where do you inherit *the feeling* that everything will be ok?
Where do you get that sense of peace from?

I have come to realize, there is a place, within each of us, that we can take ourselves to. A place that will give us that sense of peace. The kind of peace which comforts us and then, when the time is right, empowers us to chase our dreams with more determination and conviction than we could ever imagine.

Terry Gogna

Chapter 1

Crisis Creates Clarity

"The best things in life aren't things."
                                    - John Ruskin

I remember this one very special day, many years ago, where I got to experience what I call a *life clarifying* moment. On this particular day, my schedule was completely jam-packed and I believed with great conviction that there was no way that I could add anything else into my day. I had a ton of things planned and was looking forward to doing them all.

Unexpectedly the phone rang. It was a call from my nephew's family. They said my nephew had a very serious asthma attack and ruptured one of his lungs. He was taken to the intensive care unit at the hospital because the doctors said it could turn into a life or death situation at any time.

For a split second I was in a panic. I had all these appointments and things I had planned to do. I caught myself thinking reactively, *"I have no time for anything else! I'm so busy. My day is completely full."* Then all of a sudden, my conscience kicked-in and started to lead my thinking. It didn't take long to figure out what was most important and what I had to do. I cancelled all my appointments and headed straight to the hospital with my family.

When we're in the middle of a crisis, most of the time the crisis situation will force us to think with extreme creativity, simply because of the urgency of the matter. All of a sudden, we will come to realize that we have to make a decision to act in the right way quickly and correctly, otherwise the consequences could be disastrous.

The crisis situation is profound in that, when a crisis enters our life it can dramatically shift our thinking. Like removing veils from our eyes, we can instantly recognize what is truly important and what is not. All of a sudden it becomes easy to let go of things that we were holding on to, things that were taking up so much of our time. This family crisis revealed to me what

7

I truly valued deep down. It did not change my values, it simply revealed them to me with extreme clarity.

The movie 'My Life' starring Michael Keaton, portrays the crisis situation beautifully. This movie is about a man who desperately wanted to be a father. Unfortunately, when his wife finally became pregnant, he was diagnosed with terminal cancer. He was heartbroken as he thought about how his unborn son would grow up without him and without the love and support of a father. How he wouldn't be there to guide his son and contribute to making a positive difference in his life. How he wouldn't be there to comfort him and encourage him through the tough times. How he wouldn't be there to tell him how much he loved him. It was nothing less than tragic. But what made it even more painful was the fact that he was about to do the same thing to his son as his father did to him. Even though his father didn't die, all throughout his childhood he felt extreme loneliness because his father was never there for him. He would constantly hear, *"Somebody's got to make the money to put food on the table, I have to go!"* He always felt neglected by his father.

However, amid the crisis in his life he came up with an amazing idea of how he could still be a part of his son's life, even after his passing. He decided to make video messages from himself to his son. Videos that his son could watch as he was growing up. The videos contained content that he felt would be important for his son to know and experience... After his passing, every night, the boy's mother would play a video of his father reading a bedtime story to him. It was a beautiful moment for the mother when she heard her son for the very first time, recognize and speak out to his father on the TV screen, *"Dada!"* I'm sure the boy's father also experienced that very same moment in spirit.

As the boy grew older, the mother played other videos that his father was sure that he needed to see, like how to dunk a basketball, how to shave, and even how to cook spaghetti. The boy's father was determined to be a part of his son's life no matter what, even death wasn't going to stop him.

After watching this movie and being so emotionally moved, I started thinking, *"What if this happened to me? What messages would I record for my two sons?"* I couldn't get the thought out of my head. *"What would I tell my kids?"* I started thinking, if I had to do the same, not video messages, but written messages in a journal, what messages would I want to share and pass on to my kids. Not messages for children, but messages for young adults, because my boys are older. What would I write? What have I learned so far that I feel are the most important lessons, things I wish I had known earlier on in my life?

As I look back at my ancestors, it's sad to think that I had never even met my grandparents on my mother's side. They had both passed away before I was born. And my grandparents on my father's side, I only remember spending a small amount of time with them when I was 9 years old and went to India for a family vacation... that's it. My grandparents and great-grandparents and so on, all the way back in history, all those people lived for so many years, hundreds of accumulated years and I have not one piece of writing from any of them. No words. Absolutely nothing that can connect us over the ocean of years that separates us. Not one piece of writing, sharing with me, telling me directly what they experienced after living their whole life: the mistakes they made, the lessons they learned, the sacrifices they made, the things they accomplished, the traditions they followed, the principles they lived their life by, their deep personal beliefs and what they felt would be invaluable to pass on to their descendants in order for us to live a better life, a life of true fulfillment and value... but regrettably it's all lost in history. I don't say this in blame, I only say it out of sadness.

Obviously many things were passed down to me indirectly through my parents, but much more was lost, mountains of knowledge & wisdom simply evaporated. How priceless those writings would be if my ancestors had taken the time to put their life lessons on paper.

The reason words are so important is because the reader is not judging the writer, only digesting the written knowledge. Our parents can tell us to do something a dozen times before we finally accept it as truth, yet when we read it for ourselves from someone whom we've never lived with, never saw their weaknesses, never saw their flaws, we tend to accept it as truth with such little resistance.

After much reflection, I decided that I was not going to repeat the same pattern. I'm going to write in a journal the things I have learnt so far in my life, that I feel, have been the most important of lessons. And if my life was to end unexpectedly, at least my children and my grandchildren and so forth would all have access to my life lessons directly from my hands, in my words.

And so I began. I got a journal and on the top of the first page I wrote a title, *"If you are reading this, I am dead,"* and then I started writing. I wrote everything that I could recall as being important enough to want to share with my children in the unfortunate case of my unexpected death. After about 4 months I felt I had completed most of what I wanted to write for now. Then I placed the book on my book shelf with the belief & hope that if I died unexpectedly, my children would discover the book and savor each and every one of their father's messages within it.

As I walked away from the book shelf, I heard a loud voice in my head, *"Terry, you are stupid! Why are you waiting to die before your kids get this information? Tell them what is written in the book now!"*

My immediate thought was, *"That's a good idea! Why didn't I think of that?"*

After I confirmed with him that he had time to talk, I went to my older son's room and handed him the journal. *"I'd like you to read this out loud and tell me what you think."* With a very curious look on his face, he opened the book and began to read the title. *"If you are reading this, I am dead."*... *"What?!"* He started laughing out loud. *"Are you crazy?!"* I reassured him that I was not a ghost and that I titled the book this way, for a particular reason.

He found my answer both strange and amusing. When he finally calmed down after all the chuckling, he continued to read the book. *"So what do you think?"* I asked him. He told me he was very impressed with what he read and that it was definitely interesting and helpful.

10

I didn't expect him to jump up & down and rant & rave about how brilliant and life changing the content was, and that he was immediately a changed man. He wasn't even 20 years old. How much does a 20-year-old truly understand about life and its important lessons? However, I knew that as he got older, the content would become more relatable and more important to him as he referred back to it.

One of the most important things I needed to do as a parent, was to plant the best seeds I could possibly plant into the subconscious mind of my children, so that when they needed to make important decisions in the future, they could do so from a good foundation of both moral and empowering thought.

It was even more surprising to me that when I heard my son reading out loud the messages I had written in the book, the messages seemed to suddenly exhibit so much more power. As I heard them being read to me, they pierced into my mind and my heart with such validity. I was overjoyed and grateful at how important discovering these lessons had been to me in my life.

I would also encourage YOU, no matter what your age, to do the same. Take the time to write down the most important lessons that you have learnt so far in your life, that you would want to pass on to your next generation and beyond, to contribute to them having a better life. As you write down your life lessons, you will be powerfully moved by them all over again.

Be prepared also for the fact that many years later when you review your writings, what you had previously considered to be of great importance may have changed. Age and life experience is known to change our opinions on many fronts. What caused your perspective on a certain area of life to change, is now a great lesson in itself. It will make a valuable addition to your writings. Now it's time to share with you what I wrote in that book of mine. I hope the words and life lessons that follow, contribute greatly to your life and that your life becomes more abundant in all areas because of them.

Here are the *Life Lessons* of Terry Gogna...

Chapter 2

The Journey

"Let your joy be in your journey, not in some distant goal."

- Tim Cook

The dream!... The dream!... The dream!... We are always told to adamantly believe that the dream, that which we are so desperately trying to achieve, should always be our only focus, and that it should be looked upon as the trophy of our life, with the greatest of importance given to it and its attainment; for without a dream, life is completely meaningless.

What lies between our present position in life and the dream we are chasing to accomplish is the *journey*. The journey towards our dream is what we must travel and endure if we are to reach our dream. The journey holds within it, both the struggles and joys of travel, as well as the distance and time that must be weathered.

As love comes from the heart, power comes from the dream. It is our dream that empowers us to travel the journey. Our burning desire for our dream will empower us beyond measure and get us through any and all obstacles along our journey. But as powerful as our dream may be, it does not make us who we are, or determine who we become. It is the journey: the struggles, the obstacles and the challenges, that makes us who we are, and it is the attitude with which we endure through the failures, the rejection, the persecution and the heartbreaks, that ultimately determines who we become.

The journey is the foundation of *all* success. How we live our life as we chase our dream, will determine whether or not we will have joy & peace in our heart and actually feel like a success, when we finally achieve that dream. Some say, *"It doesn't matter how you get there, as long as you win; as long as you achieve your dream."* But it does matter! If you're significantly successful in one area of your life but you know you have failed in other areas and you know you have hurt people along the way including yourself, you will not feel like a success?

How you travel your journey will either add or steal joy from the success you eventually achieve. If you live your life conscientiously as you chase your dream, you will have peace in your heart instead of guilt. That peace will then empower you even further to reach higher levels of success. The journey is the foundation of your success. If you don't pay attention to the foundation and how it was constructed, i.e. how you lived your life, when it crumbles, so will your success.

The movie 'Citizen Kane' staring Orson Welles in 1941 is about a boy named Kane who was abandoned by his mother when he was a child. The boy's mother gave him away to a banker to raise, primarily to get him away from his abusive father. Many years later, after the death of his parents, at the age of 25, the boy inherited a fortune and became one of the wealthiest men in America. Even though Kane was super wealthy, unbeknownst to him, he really only had one true dream that he was chasing. He spent his entire life trying to fill the void his mother left when she abandoned him. He was desperately yearning to be loved, his heart was completely empty and desolate.

With his wealth he would purchase material things that he knew that people adored and loved with the hope of capturing that love... the love his heart was so eagerly craving. He purchased and lived in a palace on 49,000 acres of land that people loved. He filled his home with priceless collections of art that people loved. He set up a zoo on his property with animals that people loved. Yet the love still remained elusive.

As he became more and more desperate to receive and experience love, he started to push and control the people who worked for him. He wanted to be served and loved, yet paid no attention to returning any of that love he received. As a result, everyone who knew him well, despised him and literally hated his guts.

He was divorced twice. As his second wife was walking out on him, he said to her, *"Please don't go."* It looked like she was going to change her mind, until she heard his next comment, *"You can't do this to me!"*... Then she fired back, *"It's always about you and what you want!"* and continued to walk out on him, just like everybody else that ever came into his life.

On the outside, Kane looked very successful. He looked like he had made it. To people who didn't know him personally, he seemed to have it all. Everything that anyone could ever ask for, this guy had it. But his success was one dimensional. His personal life was full of regrets because he lived so thoughtlessly. He didn't pay attention to the journey, to how he lived his life, he only focused on what *he* wanted. He had all the money in the world and yet died alone and miserable on his death bed. If he had only taken the time to reflect back on his life and how he was living it, the results of his personal life would most likely have steered him into living his life a lot differently.

How you achieve your dream is just as important as the dream you achieve. Once you have travelled your journey, you can't go back and re-travel it. Do it right the first time! Live your life conscientiously. Pay attention to the journey, to all the things that are also important in your life, so you have no regrets upon achieving your ultimate goal.

If you found out that you only had six more months to live, would you all of a sudden say, "*I need to change this and this and this in my life?*" If you come to the realization that you would want to make a lot of changes to the way you live your life, that's the first clue to the fact that you are not living your life the way you should be living it.

To make my point hit home even harder, imagine that you died five minutes ago and you're standing over and looking down at your own physical body. Even though you only have a spirit body now, your mind is still intact. Nothing in your head has changed, you are still you. You still think and feel the same emotions you did a few moments earlier when you were in your physical body, but now your earthly life is over and you can't change a thing. Your life's journey is over. My question to you is this... would you have any regrets regarding how you lived your life?

Chapter 3

Relationships are the Fruit of Life

"Home is where you are loved the most and act the worst."
- Marjorie Pay Hinckley

At the end of our life, we will all come to the same conclusion, our whole life was really all about one thing, relationships. The quality of the relationships that we build on earth is truly the fruit of our life.

When my mother took her last breath and passed on into the spirit world, even though my heart was broken and my tears flowed like an endless waterfall, as I looked around the room in which she was lying, I couldn't help but feel all the love that surrounded her. So many people were crowded into that little room. Her six children gently holding her hand, or touching her face, or her legs, or her arms; we desperately wanted her to know that we were all there with her. She was not alone. We were right there beside her to see her off into the next world.

I'm sure there was no oxygen in that room, only love, pouring out of every beating heart. As I looked around, I had one overwhelming and greatly comforting thought, *"My mom did it right!"* She lived her life right and this was the fruit. The evidence was right in front of my eyes. All the love in that room was the fruit of her life, the quality of her relationships. All the love she gave out during her life was coming back to her, a thousand fold.

There are 5 relationship areas we need to pay close attention to:
1. God
2. Parents
3. Spouse
4. Children
5. Siblings and Extended Family & Friends

This list is not unique. I've come across many people who also refer to this same list of relationship areas. However, many of these people portray, in my eyes, an uncomfortable belief that this list is a hierarchy of relationship status; almost a sort of an attitude of competitiveness. I have on more than one occasion, heard a father say to his child, *"I love your mother more than I love you."* Regardless of how 'religiously' correct this hierarchy is or is not, I don't think this verbiage will help advance the relationship between a father and his child. All relationships are unique in their own right. It's not a competition, they are all important.

I learned from one of my spiritual mentors that there are 4 unique types of love, or **Realms of Heart**: The first is **Parental Love**, the love a parent gives to their child. The second is **Conjugal Love**, the love between husband and wife. The third is **Children's Love**, the love children give to their parents. And the fourth is **Sibling Love**, the love between brothers and sisters. Sibling love will eventually expand further outside of the family as the love between friends. These four types of love, or realms of heart, are unique in their own right and can only be experienced once you are in that unique position as a parent, child, spouse or sibling. Because of these unique differences, I put each relationship that I value around myself in a circle:

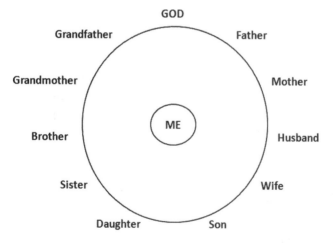

A few years ago I had a very interesting conversation with my son regarding manhood. He asked me, *"When does a boy actually become a man?"* I told him, in Western Society, when a person is 21-years-old, they are considered to be an adult and completely responsible for their own actions. However, it's not the size of your body or your age that makes you a real man or woman, it's the maturity of your heart, or what is referred to in the Bible as **perfection of heart**. Jesus said, *"Be ye therefore perfect, as your Father which is in heaven is perfect."* Only upon perfecting our heart do we become a real man or woman. But how do we do that?... by perfecting *the love* in our heart.

If God is perfect and God is also love, then in order to be perfect, one has to be perfect in love. Since there are four types of love or realms of heart, perfecting our love can only be done by experiencing and perfecting each type of love. As we perfect the love in our heart by experiencing to the full extent, each type of love, our heart will get a little closer to resembling God's heart. I truly believe that this is God's goal for each and every one of us; to one day, be able to love as God loves.

So going back to my son's question, *"When does a boy become a man?"* The answer lies in the difference between two hearts. The heart of a child vs. the heart of a parent. What separates them is the **desire within the heart.** The child thinks only of himself, where as the parent thinks only of the child. The further you get from selfish desires, the closer you get to becoming a true man or woman.

What is love? Most people will say, *"Love is a feeling, an indescribable feeling of joy and contentment in one's heart towards another human being."* Well said! Now let me ask you, when you're in the middle of a heated argument with your spouse, or you are upset with your child because of his selfish behavior towards his younger brother, how much love are you actually feeling for your spouse or your child at that very moment? I don't think you're feeling that same, *"Indescribable feeling of joy and contentment,"* that was described earlier. What happened to the feeling of love? Do you not love that person anymore now that the feeling of love has disappeared?

True Love is not a feeling. To truly love someone is to possess and express an attitude of commitment to serve and live for the sake of another, regardless of your own needs and feelings. True love is a decision to serve, rather than to be served. If we serve with an expectation of being served by the very person we are serving, it is not true love, but simply living for our own sake. We must have the attitude that, 'I don't want anything in return from this person; my kindness to this person will return to me in some other way, from some other source.' This is very hard to do, but knowing this universal law and attempting to live this way is a good starting point.

I told my son, when a person becomes mature in heart, the person chooses to put themselves at the center of their family and with an attitude of true love and commitment, serves each of the members of their family without expecting anything in return. I drew out this diagram to better illustrate my point.

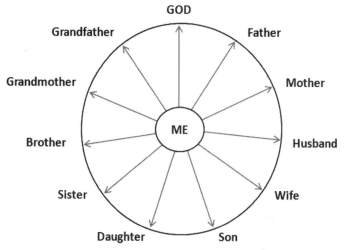

The arrows are only pointing one way. Your own needs should not come into play, your only focus should be on how you can be of service to others within your family. Your attitude is most important. You should not be serving out of fear but out of love. Fear may temporarily change your behavior but love will permanently change your heart.

"How does a person serve?", my son asked... The first priority everyday should be to stay connected in heart with God through prayer. Talk to God, but not like everyone else. Don't ask for 50,000 things like a grocery list: *"God can you help me with this and this and this and this and this and this?"* That would simply be living for your own sake.

Instead, tell God, *"I don't want anything from You except to tell me what I can do for You. I want to put a smile on Your face. I want to give You a hug. I want to tell You how much I love You. I want to tell You that I'm here for You. Please use me, guide me and direct me on how I can make this world a better place."*... Be God loving instead of God fearing.

As God listens to all the prayers around the world, to myriads of people continuously asking for things, among them, he will hear your faint voice, *"I don't want anything, just tell me what I can do for You. I want to put a smile on Your face. I want to give You a hug. I want to tell you how much I love You. I just want to tell you that I'm here for You. Please use me, guide me and direct me on how I can make this world a better place."* If you were God, how would you feel upon hearing this prayer? I'm sure God would think, *"Finally, someone I can work with to make this world a better place."*

Then I told my son, the next thing you want to do is, as often as you can, ask your grandparents, *"Is there anything I can do for you?"* Then ask your mother, *"Is there anything I can do for you?"* Then ask your father, me, *"Is there anything I can do for you?"* He chuckled. As I looked at his face, I could see he was already getting tired of all this asking, but I continued, because he was the one who wanted to know how a boy becomes a man.

"Then you should go to your younger brother and tell him, 'I'm your older brother, you can always count on me. Is there anything I can do for you?'" As I looked at my son's face, I could tell that he wasn't exactly pumped up about all this potential serving.

"So what do you think?"... *"Well, it sounds good dad, but I already know what you're going to say if I ask you, 'Is there anything I can do for you?' You're going to tell me to take the trash out, mow the lawn, shovel the snow and who knows what else!"*... *"You're mistaken! The first time you come to me and ask me, 'Is there anything I can do for you?', my answer will be, ABSOLUTELY NOTHING! You've done exactly what I hoped you would do, you have shown me that you care. However, the second time you ask me, I probably will ask you to take out the trash."*

I told my son to look at the diagram again and point out to me exactly where HE is on MY circle. *"Right here on the circumference,"* he said. *"Yes, you're right. You are on the circumference of MY circle. The day you decide to take responsibility to become a man and a leader in the family, will be the day you decide to have your own circle and put yourself in the center."*

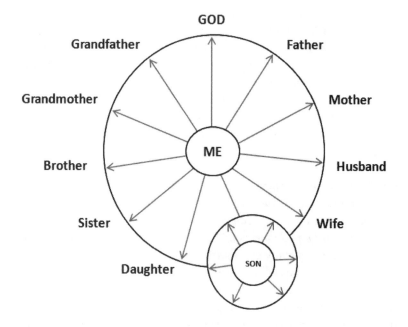

About a year ago, on a very cold winter day, it was about nine o'clock in the evening when I asked my kids if they would like to have some McDonald's to eat. They both shouted, *"Yes!"* Even though the weather outside was very cold, my younger son, who was about 19 at the time, said, *"Dad, would you like me to go and get the food?"* It was very thoughtful of him to offer. I told him, *"It's okay, I'll get it."* As I was writing down on a piece of paper what they wanted me to get for them, I kept thinking how considerate my son was to offer to go and get the food. As I looked up, I could see a big smile on my son's face... and that's when I realized, he knew what I would say if he offered to go on my behalf. He's heard this talk on a CD and knew that if he quickly asked me and showed that he cared, I would most likely say, *"It's*

okay, I'll get it." When he realized that I figured out what he just did, he burst out laughing. My son was an A+ student and now also a qualified smart-ass! At least I know he understands the philosophy of serving, even though he was using it to his own advantage.

Look carefully at the diagram on the previous page. What do these circles resemble in biology?... They look like cells with a nucleus in the center. An organism is made up of cells. The liver is made up of liver cells. The kidney is made up of kidney cells. When a person is diagnosed with liver cancer, it's because one or more of the cells of the liver have become cancerous and are starting to spread and kill the other cells.

The family is a living organism made up of cells. Each member of a family is a cell. We as cells, have a choice... are we going to be healthy cells or cancerous cells? If we choose to be a cancerous cell, we will destroy our family. If we choose to be a healthy cell, we will contribute to the growth of our family and experience joy and harmony within it. But how does one become a healthy cell?

The family is the school of love. It is within the family that we first experience love which comes from our parents and grandparents. As we experience more and more unconditional love in our childhood, that love takes root in our heart. As we grow older, we gradually begin to understand how to give that love back to our parents, grandparents, siblings and friends. It is this type of family environment that creates healthy cells.

The most influential person in any family or a group of families will always be the person who **serves** the most, **sacrifices** the most, **forgives** the most and **loves** the most. We've all heard the audacious declarations of ambitious people, *"I want to do big things and change this world for the better."* It's great that they feel this way and I only wish the best for them. However, we must understand that the change that we would like to see in this world is deeply rooted in the hearts of the people of the world. Good people will contribute to society & enhance the harmony, and bad people will destroy & create chaos... But where do good and bad people come from? They both come from families. As the family multiplies, the world will automatically change for the better or worse depending on what kind of people we are duplicating from within our families. In order to change the world, we need to ask ourselves, *"Are we a cancerous cell or a healthy cell?"* There are always exceptions to every rule, but more than likely we will duplicate what we are and what is in our hearts. Even if we have been unfortunate to come from a broken and abusive home, we can always borrow power and courage from the many heroes in society who have come from similar beginnings and chose to make a decision to no longer continue the duplication of pain, but to start the duplication of love through their own new family. The love you give to your family members will never die, it will remain in their hearts and they will then multiply it by passing it onto their children and their children's children. It will become a legacy of love.

There is however, one big challenge that we may experience with this philosophy of living for the sake of others. The challenge is this... **you can only give what you have.** If you have love in your heart then you can give love to others very easily, but what happens when we have no more love to give? What happens when we have poured out all our love unconditionally to our family members year after year and nothing comes back? Where do we get the love from to be able to keep on loving them? We must have a way to replenish the love in our hearts, otherwise we will simply become empty and tired of loving. We can only give what we have. If there's no love in our heart, we will give what remains; frustration, anger, and pain. Hurting people, will always hurt people.

Where do we get the love from?
How do we replenish it?

When a mother has a new born baby, every few hours that baby cries to be fed, *"Waa! Waa! Waa!"* Then it cries to be burped, *"Waa! Waa! Waa!"* Then it cries for its diaper to be changed, *"Waa! Waa! Waa!"* All day and all night for days the baby takes and takes from the mother. The baby only thinks of itself... *"Feed me! Burp me! Change me!"* Day after day the mother is pushed to her limits with regards to her energy and her patience. For weeks and weeks the mother continually gives of herself to the point of exhaustion. Where does the mother eventually get the energy to keep on loving her baby? For how long can she keep doing this?

Then one day, as she is up at night feeding the baby with her eyes closed, she glances down at the baby by opening just one eye and sees her baby looking up at her with its eyes wide open, those big beautiful eyes like a lake on a summers day glimmering back at her. All of a sudden, just for a second, the baby breaks a smile... and then it disappears. It's as though the baby was trying to tell her, *"Thank you!"* The mother is so overjoyed that she screams at her sleeping husband, *"Wake up! Wake up! The baby smiled! Oh my God! The baby smiled! I have the most beautiful baby in the world!"* Tears are flowing down her face in overwhelming love for her child... there's no more sleeping for her tonight. She's not tired anymore. She got all the energy she needed from that little smile of gratitude, her baby finally responded to her unconditional giving of love.

So why did that baby smile? It wasn't actually a smile at all. The baby was simply letting out gas and it caused the mouth to stretch. But let's not tell the mother. Even though I'm sure she wouldn't care what we thought, she knows what she saw and that's enough for her... *"My baby smiled, aahh."*

If I asked most men, *"How many push-ups can you do?"* most of them will have a rough estimate. *"Maybe 20, 25, or 30."* But is this really how many they are *capable* of doing?

George says, *"I can do 42."*... *"Are you sure you can't do more?"*... *"I've tried many times, the most I could do would be 43 max!"*... *"Okay, go ahead, give it everything you've got."*

George gets in position and off he goes. The first 20 are easy. The next 15 are tough, but he gets through them. Now he's at 36, 37, 38... he's not breathing much at all, using every bit of strength and focus he has... 39, 40. The veins are now popping out of his forehead. He growls out loud, *"Foooorrrrty Waaaaahn!"*... He thinks to himself, *"I knew I shouldn't have participated in this."* He's in agony and now doubt is starting to creep into every muscle of his body. It was like the actual thought of not being able to do it opened the door and doubt rushed in. It looks as though George is not even going to make it to 42. Most people would definitely bet against him at this point. Where is George going to get the power to continue the pursuit of his goal when it's obvious that he has nothing left inside of him to give?

23

There is a scene in the movie '300' where Leonidas, the leader of the Spartan army shouts out to his men, *"Spartans!!! What is your profession?!"* And all 300 men raise their spears and chant a deathly roar that would send chills down your spine, *"Arhoo! Arhoo! Arhoo!"* The beating of metal spears against their shields echoes power into the bodies of each and every warrior.

Now, let's get back to George and his push-ups. *"Foooorrrrty Waaaaahn!!!!!"* George growls in agony. *"Foooorrrrty....."* he's half way to 42, his muscles are trembling and everyone is wondering if he's even going to make it to 42. Then all of a sudden he hears the loud thundering voice of Leonidas from a clip of the movie '300'... *"Spartans!!! What is your profession?... Arhoo! Arhoo! Arhoo!"* The beating of metal spears against the shields of the Spartan warriors echoes power into every muscle of George's body... And George screams, *"42, 43, 44, 45!!!!!"*

Each night, in almost every city and country around the world, a dedicated Network Marketing entrepreneur is out showing their business plan to a prospect. He or she is determined to reach their goal of financial freedom by building their network, one ambitious person at a time. As they drive the miles to meet with their prospects in rain or snow, they sit eyeball to eyeball, expressing with compassion, their desire to help others reach their financial goals in order for they themselves to reach theirs. With great belief in their core, they pour out their hearts humbly to their prospects in order to get them to dream big dreams. They do their utmost to inspire and breathe hope into them; that there is a way and they too can achieve their dreams.

So very often, the entrepreneur after pouring out the belief in their heart, are compelled to hear the words, *"I'm not interested in your business. It's not going to work for me and I know it's not going to work for you either, you're wasting your time!"* The prospect literally takes the entrepreneur's belief and stomps on it. The entrepreneur respectfully accepts their decision and with a rejected and wounded heart, continues on with their journey.

Every time a new or mentally weak entrepreneur receives consecutive *No's*, their belief level will definitely deplete. After hearing fifteen *No's* in a row, the energy and belief of an entrepreneur may be at a dangerously low level. After experiencing *"No!"* repeatedly, where does an entrepreneur get the belief from, to continue their quest?

The belief comes from the team meetings, the conventions, the 'mass' association. Associating with the power source, the leaders who have already achieved the level of success that the entrepreneurs are attempting to achieve, this positive environment will re-empower them with belief. Association is absolute key to maintaining ones belief level. Every time you get a *"No!"* from a prospect, you have just experienced negative association. It will always drain some of your belief. Positive association will re-empower you, it will give you back the belief you need so you can keep fighting to achieve your dreams, for at least another month.

Ladies, I have a question for you!... What happens to your husband's behavior after watching a romantic movie? All of a sudden he's leaving little love notes for you on the bathroom mirror. He brings you flowers for no other reason except to say, *"I love you."* He leaves chocolates on your pillow like they do on the cruises. He starts opening the car door for you, from the outside. He starts telling you how beautiful and radiant you look. He even washes the dishes without you asking him. What has happened to your man? Where did he suddenly get all the romantic impulses from?... The movie.

So going back to the original question... *Where do we get the love from, when we feel we have no more love to give? What replenishes our love?*

Reading spiritual & positive mental attitude books and practicing meditation will definitely empower us to become a more empathetic and compassionate person. However, the greatest source of love comes from our personal relationship with God, our Heavenly Father... our Heavenly Parent. The stronger and closer our relationship is with God, the more love we will feel in our hearts. As we give love to God through prayer and doing His will, the love that He returns to us is so much more powerful than the love we gave Him. The love we receive from God has a unique quality to it in the sense that it encourages us to give it away as soon as we receive it, it literally makes us want to love another. God's love in our heart will encourage and empower us to **serve** others, **sacrifice** for others, **forgive** others and continue to **love** others.

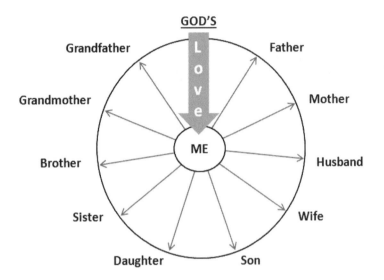

Why are relationships so important?

The **emotional hole** in the heart has killed many a spirit.

No matter how many material things we manage to ambitiously accumulate by great financial success, there is a portion of our heart that can only be filled with the love that comes from relationships. If it remains empty, it will become an emotional hole in our heart. There are numerous examples of financially successful people that have turned to drugs & alcohol to fill the void that aches inside of them. We must consider the development of reciprocal loving relationships in themselves, as a very high level of achievement, since the attainment of such relationships will not only give us joy and inner peace, but will empower us to achieve greater success in all other areas of life.

I always wondered, upon our death...

What is the most valuable 'thing' we can leave behind on this earth? Do we really get to take nothing with us to the spirit world?

I have discovered and deeply hold the belief that the answer to the two questions above is the exact same answer.

The most valuable thing we can leave behind on this earth is love. The love we give to others not only lives forever in the hearts of our loved ones, but will continue to multiply and empower all those who receive it to do the same. It is only the love we leave behind that will make this world a better place than what it was when we departed.

I have heard many people say, *"You can't take anything with you when you die."* This assumption is absolutely false. There is something you can take with you... **love**. Not only can you take the love you received from others, but more importantly you can also take, in a profound way, the love you gave to others... The more love you have given to others during your life on earth, the more love you will get to take with you to the spirit world.

Chapter 4

Marriage and More

"My wife and I were happy for twenty years, then we met."

- Rodney Dangerfield

As an International Speaker, I have spoken to Network Marketing entrepreneurs all over the world. In regards to building their businesses as a couple, I tell them all the same thing, *"If you have a great marriage, it may not necessarily help you to build your business faster and achieve the high levels of success you desire, but I can tell you one thing for sure, if you have a poor relationship it will definitely affect your business negatively."*

I've been married for almost 30 years and it took many years into my marriage for me to realize something that today, seems so stupidly obvious. Every time I had an argument with my wife, the argument would not only affect me negatively, but it would negatively affect every area of my life. It would literally suck out every ounce of energy that I had, to the point where I couldn't get myself to do anything except sit around and watch television all day long.

However, every time things were going great in our relationship, not only did the relationship positively affect every area of my life, but more importantly, it empowered me personally, making me feel like I could do anything because I had the support and encouragement from the person who's support and encouragement mattered to me the most. I could have dozens of people tell me that they're behind me but when my wife says it, that's when it really makes the difference.

After years of good times, then bad times, then good times, then bad times and on and on, I started thinking seriously about what I could do to prevent the arguments so we could have longer periods of good times in our relationship. I really felt that if I did nothing and just let things run their course, it would only get worse.

We never had arguments when we first got married; we seemed to come to an agreement on everything... *"Honey, where would you like to go to eat?"...* *"Wherever you want to go is fine with me."...* *"Well, wherever you want to go is fine with me."*

Six months later... *"Honey, let's go to Red Lobster."...* *"We always go to Red Lobster! Why can't we go somewhere else?"*

What changed all of a sudden?... The first 6 to 18 months of a marriage usually goes well because each partner is lovingly focused on the other's needs. They have blind love for one another. Their goal is primarily to make their spouse feel special; loving them by serving them. They literally live for the other person's sake while putting aside their own needs and wants. But then somewhere after 6 to 18 months, one or both partners begin to get tired of serving the other's needs, especially if their own needs are not being met. From that point on, their marriage starts going downhill. The relationship will either end in divorce, or they will rescue it, if they can figure out what is going wrong and agree to make the necessary changes in their behavior towards each other. Their determination and willingness to make the necessary changes in their behavior will largely depend on their personal definition of marriage. What they believe marriage to be will now determine their attitude & resolve towards putting out the effort and making their marriage a success or not.

I'm going to share with you a few things I've learned over almost 30 years of marriage, things I've learned and *still apply*. I hope these nuggets will also contribute to your relationship.

(1) Understanding Your Spouse

I started reading educational books on relationships and personalities. Books such as 'Positive Personality Profiles - D.I.S.C.' by Robert Rohm and 'Five Love Languages' by Gary Chapman. These were excellent resources. They helped tremendously. Robert Rohm talks about the fact that there are four personality types: Dominant, Inspiring, Cautious and Supportive. Most people will be a combination of their two strongest traits. For example, a person could be *Dominant & Cautious (DC)* or *Dominant*

29

& Inspiring (DI). The most important part of this information is that if you know what personality type your spouse is, you will have more success in communicating with them because you can talk to them in a way their personality type best receives communication.

Gary Chapman talks about the five love languages: *Words of Affirmation, Acts of Service, Receiving Gifts, Quality Time and Physical Touch.* He teaches that a person will only feel completely loved when you love them in their unique love language. For example, if you keep buying gifts for someone to show how much you love them, they still may not feel loved if that is not their love language. If their love language is *Physical Touch,* holding their hand or hugging them would make them feel more loved than receiving gifts.

These kinds of books helped me to better understand my wife and why she behaved the way she did, and most importantly, be able to predict her behaviour. I desperately needed this information because it seemed like when I married her I had one eye closed and then after 6 to 18 months my other eye slowly opened and I started seeing all her faults. I'm sure it was the same for her too. They don't call it **blind love** for no reason.

(2) Understanding Yourself

The greatest change for me however, came from reading personal growth books on **attitude, character and spirituality**. These books taught me to stop looking at my wife's behavior and focus instead on myself. It was as though the words in these books were pleading with me, *"Wake up! Look inside yourself, the answer is there. If you want your marriage to become better you need to make your heart right. Change your heart!... The problem is your heart, not your wife!"*

I still remember the day many years ago, when I took responsibility and made the decision to work on my marriage. The first thing I did was to start recording discretely all of my wife's complaints. Every time she complained about something I did or did not do, I wrote it down on a piece of paper:

"The sink is full of dirty dishes!"
"You left your underwear on the floor again!"
"The kitchen's a mess!"
"The garbage bin is full!"

Every time she complained, I wrote it down. After a couple of days I thought to myself, *"I'm going to need a bigger piece of paper."*

After a week I noticed something strange. My wife wasn't actually complaining about 100 different things. It was the same 5 or 6 things coming up over and over again. It just seemed like a hundred because I wasn't taking care of them fast enough.

After a couple of weeks, I basically knew what all the complaints were. I decided to set a goal to eliminate each of them one by one before they became a complaint.

Because I was focusing on my wife's needs, I was successful in eliminating almost all of her complaints. Unfortunately, there was still one complaint that I couldn't eliminate. My wife will just have to live with that one because I'm not going to the veterinarian any time soon... I'm sure you can figure out what that complaint was. I'll leave it to your imagination!

(3) **Victimhood**

My wife and I used to have so many arguments early on in our marriage and whenever I found myself blaming her for our bad relationship it made me feel like a victim. I would think to myself...

"It's all her fault! She's going to cause us to have a divorce. Why doesn't she understand what she's doing wrong?"

The more I blamed her, the more I felt like a powerless victim. The choice of whether we had a successful marriage or not, I believed, was in her hands. Everything changed when I changed my attitude and decided to take responsibility for my marriage. I came to a profound realization... My wife is a **product of my behavior**. If I behave a certain way, she behaves a

31

certain way. If I change my behavior, her behavior will automatically change. This epiphany gave me the power and belief that I could actually create the marriage I want, instead of hoping that it would turn out okay by chance. This power subsequently came from an attitude change, which originated from a heart change.

(4) <u>Choose Your Battles Wisely</u>

As I looked back at what we were constantly arguing about, to me the arguments were over so many silly little insignificant things like dishes left in the sink or underwear left on the floor. What's the big deal? They were nothing, yet she was starting World War III over them. I realized something HUGE, they weren't *little* to her. They really bugged her. They were signs to her of how inconsiderate I was being because I was the one making the mess and expecting her to clean it up. Let me give you an example. This is what she felt I was saying, when I left my underwear on the floor...

"My dear sweet wife, I am the King of this house. This is my underwear. I am leaving it here on the floor for you because I am too busy and you have nothing to do all day. I am blessing you with the honor of picking up my holy underwear, raising it above your head in respect and gently placing it in the laundry basket. Thank you, my slave."

This is definitely not what I was thinking when I left my underwear on the floor, but I guess it doesn't really matter what I was thinking. The only thing that mattered is how my wife interpreted my behavior and how it caused her to feel. I learned a big lesson. I can't influence the way my wife interprets my behaviour, but I can change my behaviour. After learning this valuable lesson, I started choosing my battles more wisely.

When the house was neat and tidy, my wife became the girl I married, a sweet, gentle, little angel. When I left my underwear lying on the floor, she would change into a monster. The choice of who I wanted to live with was in my hands. From that day on, I decided to never leave my underwear on the floor, it went straight into my pocket first as I got up, never mind the laundry basket.

Every time I put a dish in the sink and was about to walk away, thinking about the consequences brought me right back to the sink. As I washed the dishes I would motivate myself by singing, *"Beautiful, sweet, gentle angel. I don't want a monster in my house."*

I remember later in that same week, I was in the kitchen when my son walked passed me with some dirty dishes. He put them in the sink and began walking away. *"Hey, where are you going?!... Upstairs... I know you're going upstairs, but why aren't you washing your dirty dishes?... Oh, I'm busy doing something... So who's suppose to wash your dishes?... Umm, well, mom or you, I guess?... Stand over here for a second and let me show you what you're really saying to your mom and I by your actions."*

"I am the Prince of this house. These are my dirty dishes. I am way too busy to wash them myself. I am leaving them in the sink for my mother or my father to wash, because they don't have anything better to do. Thank you, my slaves."

"That's not what I'm saying, Dad."... "It doesn't matter what you're not verbally saying, your actions are saying it for you."

That was the last time he left his dirty dishes in the sink. Instead he started leaving them in his bedroom. He had piles of dirty dishes on his bed. But eventually each night he would come down and wash them all at one time. He did finally learn the lesson. He understood that his actions were sending out a non-verbal message regardless of his real intentions.

(5) The Danger Zone

When my wife and I were newly married, our relationship was full of curiosity, excitement, adventure, fun and surprise. Everything was a new experience. But I have to be honest with you, after 20 years, there wasn't much curiosity left. Things got pretty boring because everything was so predictable. No adventure and no surprise. This is a very dangerous stage for a relationship to get into. Luckily, we realized this and decided to spice things up a bit. There were two things my wife and I agreed to do that made a huge difference: The first was *Surprise Dating*. We would both take turns each month to set up a date for the other. This brought back the surprise, the fun and the adventure because neither one of us knew what the other had planned. All we could do was look forward to it.

The second thing we did was for each of us to have a 'Girls Night Out' and a 'Boys Night Out', respectively. I realized many times that when my wife went out with her girlfriends, she had an absolutely great time, totally different than when she went out with me. With the girls, after she came home and told me some of the stories of what had happened, she would giggle like crazy, *"hehehe!"* She never giggled like this when she was with me. And so I always encouraged her to go out and have fun with the girls. I would think to myself, *"Go and giggle as much as you can my dear. Have fun and then come home happy, to me."* It was better than wine. It always worked out great.

(6) Always Be The First To Say Sorry

When I got married, I thought I was marrying a sweet, gentle, little angel. After a few months I got a big surprise. She was not as gentle as she looked. This little girl was as fierce as a tiger... *"Wehhhh!!!"*

Anytime we had an argument, she would stop talking to me. First for a day... then it turned into 2 days... then 3 days... then 4 days... sometimes she didn't talk to me for a week. The girl was crazy!!! I would ask her, *"How many days are you going to keep this up and not speak to me?"*... *"It wasn't my fault!"* she would say.

She was so much more stubborn than me. She would never say sorry no matter what, even if there was a slight chance that it might be her fault. I do have to admit though, 99% of the time it was my fault, but still, a week without talking, that's a hefty sentence for anybody. She could pass for a monk that was taking a vow of silence! Just kidding. Don't tell her I said that, otherwise she'll stop talking to me again!

After experiencing so many silent treatments over the years, I figured out that if I want to shorten or even end these episodes, I better learn to apologize regardless of who's fault it is. Not talking to each other in a marriage is very dangerous, especially if you're married to someone who is competitive. There's no reward for the person who can stay silent the longest.

I decided I was going to say sorry first, every time we had an argument, even if it was her fault. Years later on this one particular day, for the first time, she quietly said to me, *"I'm sorry."*... Oh my God! I got on my knees, stretched out my arms with my palms facing up to the heavens and shouted out in gratitude, *"Thank you God!"* It was a miracle from heaven when I heard those sweet little words.

A beautiful thing happened that day: I realized there were only so many times that I had to continuously say *"I'm sorry"* before my wife began to also say it. Today even if we argue, we don't stop talking to each other for longer than an hour or so. *Sorry* is a very important word in a marriage. It's like glue, so we keep it handy and use it often.

I told my kids the best thing you can do if your parents are mad at you, especially me, your dad, is to as quickly as possible say *sorry*. It will deflate the anger as fast as air coming out of a balloon. But to say sorry is a very difficult thing for the majority of people to do, because when it is needed the most, it totally contradicts the emotions that we are feeling inside. Both parties strongly believe and feel that they are right, so why should either of them say sorry? Each has the mind-set that whoever says sorry first, loses. This mind-set is the problem. It should not be about winning or losing in a relationship, it should be all about harmony and keeping the peace.

If you want peace in your marriage and in your family, don't be too proud to say sorry. It takes more courage and a more loving heart to say sorry, than to not talk. Being alone in silence is not winning. Just say sorry!

(7) Join Your Spouse's World

The movie 'What Dreams My Come' is about a couple who lost both of their teenage children in a car accident. The mother was overwhelmed with grief. The pain of losing her children had reached the pinnacle and literally ripped her heart in two. She fell into a nervous breakdown and ended up in a psychiatric hospital after trying to commit suicide. Her husband was extremely loyal and would visit her as often as he could at the hospital. During one of those visits, his wife dropped a bombshell on him...

"I think we should have a divorce... What are you saying?... We're too different. For one, why didn't you go crazy too?! Your children died!... I know. I remember the silence in the house. I thought I had to be strong for the both of us... For me?"

All of a sudden, the husband realized what he did wrong. He knew he had to be strong for his wife, but the definition of *strong* in his mind meant *to not show emotion*. To break down emotionally in the presence of his wife would be to absolutely fail in being a man. He believed maintaining a stoic composure reflected the strength his wife would need and could rely on, if and when she broke down.

Even though he desperately wanted to win over the pain that he himself was fighting against, he came to the realization that he was wrong to believe that the only way to win was to show no emotion. His real fight was not against the pain, but to stay connected to his wife's heart.

"I pushed the pain away so hard that I disconnected myself from the person I loved the most. Sometimes when you win, you lose. Because I couldn't join you, I left you alone, alone to handle the grief by yourself."

The greatest lesson I learnt from this movie was that the secret to developing a great relationship is to leave your world and join your partner in theirs. If the husband openly grieved in front of his wife, she would have felt a deep desire to comfort him even in her sorrow, just as he would have comforted her. The desire to comfort each other would have pulled their hearts together into the same world.

I have 2 boys and for years I used to ask myself, *"How does a parent develop a really close relationship with their child?"* After watching this movie I finally got the answer... **join their world**.

Before I saw this movie I didn't realize, but I was always trying to get my children to join *my* world, to see the world like I saw it. I believed that if I could help them to see the world like I saw it, they would be so grateful to me that they would want to be closer to me. But this strategy does not work if you are trying to build a close relationship with children.

It's a well known fact that if you want someone to like you, you need to show interest in *them* instead of trying to get them to be interested in you. The same applies to your children. If you want them to *like* you, you must show interest in them. How do you do this?... Join their world!

Joining our child's world is not easy. As the parent, our world is always the same, we live in the Parents World. But when it comes to our children, their world keeps changing as they get older. If we don't understand this fact, we will still be treating the 10-year-old like a 5-year-old and the 15-year-old like they were still 10.

When my older son was 16, I made a decision to *join his world*. I knew his passion was basketball, so that was the world I needed to join. I told my son that I'm going to take up basketball and I would like him to teach me how to play. You should have seen the look on his face, he had a grin from ear to ear... *"Dad, you really want to play?"*... *"Yes, but I need your help. I want you to be my coach. You tell me what to do and I'll do it."* I threw the basketball to my son and yelled, *"Let's go!"* He started showing me how to dribble, how to defend and how to score. He was absolutely loving it. The look on his face told me exactly where I was... I was in HIS world.

I remember this one particular day when my wife and I were watching a TV show and my younger son entered the room to see what we were watching. He quietly took a seat but said nothing. A few minutes later at the commercial break, my wife decided to get a drink from the kitchen. As soon as she was out of the room my son whispered, *"Dad, do you like this show?"* I whispered back, *"Not really."*... *"I know why you're watching it."* I leaned over towards him with great curiosity and asked, *"Why?"* He whispered back even more quietly, *"You're trying to join Mom's world."* I couldn't believe he said this to me. Obviously he had heard one of my CDs. All I could say back to him was, *"Stop being a smart ass!"* He knew he was right because I couldn't stop grinning.

A little while after I watched the movie 'What Dreams May Come,' I decided to do a little exercise that would help me to better understand my wife's world. I began to write down all the things I could think of that my wife did on a daily basis and all the things I thought she might be stressed out about. I wanted to feel what she felt. I wanted to experience the things she experienced on a daily basis so I could understand her world. Here's just a little of what I discovered...

On most evenings my wife usually went to bed at the same time I did, close to midnight. In the morning she would get up way before I did, so she always had less sleep. She made lunches for the kids and then went to work. During the week she: cooked dinner, washed the dishes, helped the kids with their homework, did the laundry, cleaned the house, did the vacuum, took the garbage out and put the kids to bed.

The list was getting bigger and bigger. On top of all these things my wife was doing, every month she had to put up with stomach cramps and headaches due to lack of iron, as most women often do at their time of the month. As I was writing this down, I was thanking God that I wasn't a woman.

To stack the deck even more, before my wife and I got married she agreed that it would be okay for my retired parents to live in the same house with us. It was as though, as she was putting a ring on my finger, she was also putting one on her father-in-law's finger and one on her mother-in-law's finger. It was like a package deal. She was getting 3 for the price of 1. My wife had never lived in a home where she was the only woman in charge. She gave up her privacy for over 25 years only because she respected and loved me. Only after I had made this list did I truly discover what a wonderful woman I was married to.

It says in the Bible, *"Wives respect your husbands. Husbands love your wives."* I was doing it wrong... I didn't understand that *to love* includes *to respect.* I thought I was loving my wife when I said, *"I love you honey, by the way, here's my underwear."* I loved my wife, but I realized, I was not respecting her.

After I made this list, my eyes opened to how much my wife was actually doing and sacrificing in our marriage. I came to the realization that she deserved all the respect I could give her. I was married to an amazing woman with such a big heart and didn't even realize it!

I would suggest to all the husbands reading this book, to also make that list, and when you do, you too will discover what a wonderful woman you are married to. If you have difficulty coming up with things to write, I am sure your wife will help you make that list a little bigger!

(8) Half-Blind

A couple of years ago I was in my bathroom shaving and as I was drying my face I began reading the label on a hair spray can. As I was reading, I noticed the end of the sentence was on the other side of the can and I couldn't see what it said from where I was standing. My wife was also in the bathroom putting on her makeup. She was on the other side of the can, so I asked her, *"What does it say on the first line?"* As she read it to me, that's when I realized something amazing. Without my wife I would not have been able to see the other side... *without our spouse we are half-blind*. We need each other to see the whole picture. Even though your spouse thinks and sees the world differently than you, you must learn to respect your spouse's point of view, otherwise you will stay half-blind. We should expect and hope that our spouse's point of view is different than ours, so that we can get the bigger picture of a situation before a decision has to be made, no matter how difficult it would be to hear. As a couple, we can become so much more powerful if we take advantage of our different viewpoints willingly.

(9) Movies: *'Pursuit of Happyness'* vs. *'Cinderella Man'*

When the tough times came in their marriage what did each of the couples do?... In the movie 'Pursuit of Happyness,' when the tough times came financially, the wife gave up. She got up and left. She abandoned her husband and her son at the time they needed her the most. I'm not saying she wasn't justified in leaving her husband, I'm simply saying, walking away from a problem doesn't solve it, especially when there's a child in the picture. In the movie 'Cinderella Man,' when the tough times came financially, the wife did not leave. She stood beside her husband and her 3 children. She chose to support her husband regardless of how painful their situation became.

Only when you are tested through tough times and hardships within your marriage will you have the chance to prove your true value as a life partner. It's easy to support your spouse when things are going smooth, but the truly great husbands and wives are the ones who are there for their spouse when the tough times come... that's what makes them great.

(10) Movie - 'Roots'

The greatest words I've ever heard a husband say to his wife, I heard in a movie called 'Roots.' This is a movie about slavery. Chicken George became a free man when the law changed in his hometown. Unfortunately, his wife & children had to remain as slaves, as they were from a different state that still had the old law in place. The couple encountered a heartbreaking dilemma. If the husband stayed with his family he would lose his freedom and return to being a slave, but in order to be a free man he would have to leave the town in which his wife and children were enslaved. He and his wife had to make the hardest decision of their married life. They both decided that it would be best for the husband to leave to be a free man, make something of himself and then return when the law hopefully changed in his wife's hometown. So with great pain & sorrow, George reluctantly left his wife and children.

Many years later, old Chicken George was finally able to return to his family. On the very first night, as he lay next to his wife in bed, he began to hear her crying. When he asked her why she was crying, she replied, *"When you left many years ago, I was young and beautiful. Today, I'm old and wrinkled, and I'm afraid you won't love me anymore."* His response was simply heartwarming. *"Woman, I don't see you with my eyes, I see you with MY HEART."*

When you make that list to better understand your wife's world, you too will start seeing your wife with your heart.

The root of most marriage problems begins with this common belief: *"If my spouse treated me better, then I would treat them better."* This is a stalemate! If no one acts, the marriage is doomed.

So, who should act first?...

YOU should!

Chapter 5

Always Chase Your Passion

"The two most important days in your life are,
the day you are born and the day you find out why."
- Mark Twain

For years I used to ask myself, *"What am I supposed to be doing with my life?... What is my purpose?... Why am I here?"*

Today, I truly believe the number one purpose of our lives is to discover and chase our true passion. The passion I am referring to is not just one singular item. I believe we can have more than one true passion because we have more than one facet to our lives.

We can be truly passionate about our job, or why we are building a particular business and at the same time, truly passionate about our health, and at the same time truly passionate about the relationships we have with our children, our spouse and with God. I've had many people say, *"You're right, but what is your major passion?"* My answer is always the same, *"I have a major passion in each area of my life."*

Planted inside each and every one of us are dormant seeds of passion eager to germinate, but like all seeds, they will only grow in the right environment. Exposure to the correct elements is essential for the seed to release the passion within it. The only path by which these seeds of passion can receive life is through our senses. As we place ourselves in different environments, experiencing new things, what we see, hear, touch, feel, smell and taste ultimately gives life to the seed. Through stimulation of one or multiple senses simultaneously, like love at first sight, a connection is made between the element and a respective seed.

Once that connection is solidified by intensity of experience, a path is created along which energy travels from the element to the seed. As the seed receives energy from the element, it begins to vibrate. As it vibrates, the energy intensifies and spreads to the rest of our body. We can sense this in different ways: goose bumps... our heart beats faster... the hairs on the back of our neck stand up... tears begin flow. These are some of the clues to the passion that lies within. Pay attention to what makes you cry, to what gives you goose-bumps, to what captures your attention, to what you can't stop thinking about. The seeds of passion are trying to make you aware of their presence, don't ignore them!

How do you know if you've found your true passion?

There is a great scene in the movie 'Meet Joe Black' that depicts brilliantly how one would know if they have discovered their true passion when it comes to finding a life partner. The following is a conversation between a father and his daughter:

F: *"Do you love Drew?"*
D: *"You mean, like you loved Mom?"*
F: *"Forget about me and your Mom. Are you going to marry him?"*
D: *"Probably."*
F: *"Listen, I'm crazy about the guy. He's smart, he's aggressive, he could carry Parish Communications into the 21st Century and me along with it."*
D: *"So what's wrong with that?"*
F: *"That's for me. I'm talking about you... It's not what you say about Drew, it's what you don't say."*
D: *"Maybe you're not listening."*
F: *"Oh yes I am... There's not an ounce of excitement, not a whisper of a thrill. This relationship has all the passion of a pair of titmice. I want you to get swept away out there! I want you to levitate! I want you to sing with rapture and dance like a dervish!"*
D: *"Oh, that's all?"*
F: *"Yeah. Be deliriously happy!... Or at least leave yourself open to be."*
D: *"Okay, be deliriously happy?... I shall do my utmost."*
F: *"I know it's a cornball thing, but love is passion! Obsession! Someone you can't live without. I say, fall head over heels, find someone you can love like crazy and who will love you the same way back... How do you find him? Well, you forget your head and you listen to your heart. I'm not hearing any heart, cause the truth is honey, there's no sense living your life without this. To make the journey and not fall deeply in love. Well, you haven't lived a life*

43

at all. But you have to try, because if you haven't tried, you haven't lived. Stay open. Who knows, lightening could strike. "

Once you discover your true passion, you won't be able hold yourself back, you will be continuously nudged from within to chase it. Listen to that inner voice and chase your passion with everything you've got, because your true passion will lead you down a road that will eventually reveal your purpose in life. If you're thinking, *"What if I have more than one true passion like you said earlier on. How will that affect my overall purpose in life?"...* If you discover that you have more than one true passion in different areas of your life, you'll be amazed at how your passions somehow work together to lead you to the same one major purpose. However, also keep in mind, there is no law against having more than one purpose in your life!

Once you discover your purpose in life, it is through that purpose that you will make your contribution. You will contribute to your own personal growth and development first. As you struggle, battle, fail numerous times and still continue to fight with an attitude of raw determination, you will grow both mentally and emotionally. It is your passion, the desire to achieve your dream, that gives you power and it is by overcoming your challenges, that you gain wisdom.

As you grow and succeed further, you will contribute to your family next, then to your community and then possibly even to the world, depending on how hard and for how long you keep chasing your passion. The bigger your dream, the bigger your contribution. The contribution you make will eventually become your legacy. People who fail to discover their passion are usually bored with their lives. People who fail to chase their passion fail to find their purpose in life and as a result will make little or no contribution to themselves or anyone else and leave no legacy. Once they are gone, there is little evidence that they even lived.

When you discover your true passion, you won't need to worry about your confidence, it will naturally pour out of you. Your burning desire will create confidence within you. Low confidence is simply a sign that you haven't found your true passion yet. So, how do you find your true passion?... You have to actively search for it. If you're having trouble discovering your true passion, look in areas of your life that you have never looked in before. Look into the lives of great men and women that you admire. There is a reason you admire them. Your passions may be intertwined.

When you witness a super-high achiever in your profession or field of passion being recognized on stage for their achievement, what thoughts come into your mind? What are you thinking as they walk on that stage and receive their award? Have you ever had these thoughts?...

"I'm better dressed than them... I've got nicer hair than them... I can walk more gracefully than them... I can talk better than them... I can easily do what they've done... I'm going to reach that level faster than them... I'm going to break their record!"

It's easy to say that when you look at people from the outside. But what you see on the outside is not what made them a success. From the outside...

You can't see the true passion burning deep down in their heart!
You can't see the struggles and challenges they were buried under!
You can't see the pain they went through!
You can't see the tears they cried!
You can't see the times when they got knocked down on their knees again and again, and they wanted to quit so badly, but somehow they were able to get the power from within, to get themselves up and continue chasing their dream!

What is embedded deep inside a person's heart is what makes that person a success, not what you can see on the outside. So, my question to you is this... When life knocks you down, when the struggles and challenges seem to be so great & overwhelming, where are you going to get the power from to get yourself up and moving?

Are you going to be able to get yourself up like the high achievers did? I'm not talking about *not quitting*, I'm talking about getting yourself up and chasing your passion. Anyone can say, *"I'm not going to quit!"* The question is, how are you going to get yourself up when you get knocked down?! If you don't know what your true passion is, when things get tough you will stop, regardless of how pumped up you think you are right now. Anybody can beat their chest when they're excited in a crowd. But when you get hammered by rejection and doubt and you're all alone with your thoughts, where are you going to get the power from to continue to beat your chest in defiance of failure?

A few years ago, my younger son came to me complaining about school. *"Dad, why do I have to do so many different subjects at school. Why can't I just pick three that I really like and just do those?"* I told him, *"The teachers don't know where or what your true passion is. They are trying to help you discover it, by exposing you to as many different subjects as they can."*

Over the years I have coached many Network Marketing entrepreneurs and sales professionals. Most of the new recruits, after a few weeks of training from their mentors, know exactly what they should be doing in order to become successful. The challenge so many of them face is not that they don't know *what* to do, it's that they don't know how to get themselves to do it consistently.

In the Network Marketing industry, most of the time when you ask a married man, *"Why are you building your Network Marketing business?"* His response will often be, *"I want to help retire my wife out of her job. I want her to be free."* This loyal husband and entrepreneur goes out night after night determined to achieve his goal. He shows the business plan to new prospects over and over continuously for 2 months and then suddenly stops. He doesn't realize why or how he has lost momentum. He doesn't understand why the dream of freeing his wife from her job has lost its power.

The truth is, for most men, that's exactly what it is, just *a* dream, but not... *the* dream. It was not *his* true passion. It was simply a noble gesture, to free his wife from her job. Yet even though it was just a noble gesture, it did have power, power enough to drive the husband to be super active for up to two months. But why not longer?... As we continually read personal growth books, listen to CDs and attend educational seminars, we will grow and change on the inside; how we think, speak and act will be different three months from today. As a snake sheds its skin, we too will shed our old self and be a new person of better habits and character, as we keep on this path of education.

It is very important to understand. As we change on the inside, there's a very good chance that our dreams and passions will also change. What inspired and drove us to super activity six months ago may no longer empower us today. We need to be aware of the power of our true passion. If we find ourselves slowing down or losing our drive, we must take the time to search out for a new passion. For many individuals, discovering their true passion or dream is more difficult than actually achieving it, once it is discovered.

It is a common fact that all huge leaders in the Network Marketing industry endorse and promote an activity they call *Dream-Building*. This is an activity that is entirely dedicated to the purpose of searching out one's real dream or true passion. But one major thing must be kept in mind, our true passion is not always a visible entity. Many times it is hidden deep in one's heart and must be laboriously mined. Just like digging for gold and gems, many times we will think we have found what we were looking for, only to be disappointed because it was not the real thing.

The power of one's true passion once discovered, is invaluable. In the Network Marketing industry if you help a teammate discover their true passion, your work to keep them motivated is over, they will be virtually unstoppable. Over the years, I have discovered 12 different types of dreams or passions. I call them *Strategic Formulas*. When one formula loses its power and no longer inspires super activity, the switch to another formula becomes absolutely necessary. These formulas are sources of power. When life knocks us down, the power we need to get ourselves up and moving, will most likely come from one of these 12 formulas.

Here is Formula #1...

Chapter 6

Power of the Material Dream
(Formula #1)

"Everything great was accomplished by fools who dreamed."
- Testy McTesterson

There are many people who absolutely love sports cars. In fact, when they see a beautiful Porsche, Ferrari or Lamborghini roaring down the street, their heart begins to race and for a brief moment through their imagination, they are transported to another world. A world where they alone are king of the road and master of the gas guzzling beast. Behind the wheel they can feel the power of a wild animal in their hands. Will it be too strong or will they be able to tame it? This is the only thing on their mind... *"Roar! Roar!"... "Easy boy!"...* They are completely consumed by the car's power & beauty. Their dream of becoming one with this mighty machine becomes a reality for a brief moment.

Every business leader will tell you how absolutely vital it is to get a picture of your dream car, your dream home, your dream vacation, your dream boat, your dream watch, your dream plane or whatever your material dream is and put it up on your wall so you can be inspired by its beauty and the visual power it exudes every time you look at it. Your desire and deep hunger for it will radiate power to you and consistently push you into the action that results in its achievement.

George's dream car is a Ferrari. He truly believes that one day he will own his own Ferrari. He has his eye on a red 458 Spider with a retractable hard-top. 419KW of power, 0 to 100km/h in 3.4 seconds with a maximum speed of 320km/h. George gets the best picture he can find and puts it up on his office wall. He steps back, takes a deep breath, holds it, stares at his future car and then slowly lets out a sigh of deep desire, *"Ahhhhhh."*

Every day as he enters his office, George leans over to the picture of his dream car and kisses it... *"You'll be mine soon baby."* About a week later, George enters his office, he looks at the picture of his dream car and salutes it, *"You'll be mine soon baby. "*... He didn't kiss it this time. Only a salute. A few days later, as George enters his office, he looks up at the picture of his Ferrari and smiles... No kiss and no salute. A few weeks later, George enters his office, goes straight to his desk and begins his work... he didn't kiss the picture of his Ferrari, he didn't salute it, he didn't even smile at it. In fact, he didn't even notice it was there anymore. Magically it had turned into wallpaper. The picture of the Ferrari, the picture of his dream, had lost its power.

It is very important to understand that the true sustainable power does not come from a picture... the true power comes from the experience.

George needs to go to the Ferrari dealership and experience, as fully as he can, the *personality* of his dream. It's the personality that he needs to connect and become one with, not just the look. He needs to open the door of that car and slide into the stitched leather bucket seats. As he closes the *vault*, he needs to feel the deep cushioned thud in his ear drums. He needs to take a slow deep breath in through his nostrils and smell the quality leather that he's encapsulated within. He needs to take a moment and enjoy the beauty of the lights, the colours, the contours and the immaculate details of the inside of the car. He needs to slide his fingertips across the dash and feel the smooth, rich essence of the surface. He needs to take a forceful grip of the gear stick and hold it there, allowing the power of the sleeping engine to seep into every artery of his body until it is eventually pumped into his heart. As he hears and feels the roar of the engine deep within, he becomes one with his dream.

As George lets go of the gear stick, he suddenly disconnects himself from the power source. He reaches for the door handle, pushes open the vault and reluctantly slides out of the car. He sadly walks away from his dream car and heads towards the car he currently owns. As he gets into his rust-bucket and shuts the door, he immediately experiences the shock of a complete drop in quality. As the door closes it sounds more like the rattle of a tin can. The new car smell had turned into *old hamburger* smell and half of the lights on the dash didn't work. George slowly lowered his head in shame and let out a deep sigh. A tear slid down his cheek as he felt his heart break. He so longed to be back in the arms of his dream car. Right at that very moment, George vowed that he would never give up on his dream and would be back to claim what he knows is his destiny.

When a person experiences their material dream intimately, the emotion from that experience gets inside the heart of the person and stirs their soul. Their new born passion then begins to drive them to accomplish spectacular feats of activity. Quitting is no longer an option. They will keep fighting until they eventually achieve their dream.

Even though there are many beautiful material dreams in the world to aspire towards, there are a select group of individuals who strongly believe and promote that desiring a material dream is immoral. They proudly confess that they are righteous because they refuse to chase a material object.

"It's not right to dream about Ferraris and mansions when there are so many starving children around the world."

They say this with such compassion as they sit back in their recliner and continue to flick between the channels on their television. The sad thing about a lot of these people is that, not only are they doing nothing to help the starving people of the world, but they are also discouraging others from chasing and achieving their material dream through a false preaching of guilt.

Some of these people who say it's wrong, secretly deep down in their own heart would love to own a Ferrari, but they choose to wrestle with their passion and continue to believe, *"It's wrong!"* They simply will not allow themselves to get excited about any material dream. And so many of them, while they confess their motivation is to feed the poor, can't even get themselves off the couch.

Having a passion to own a dream car or a passion to feed the poor are both, in their own right, great aspirations. There is nothing wrong with either of them. The thing we need to understand is that there is a reason and a purpose to chasing a passion. The passion or the dream we are chasing has one significant overall purpose... to give us power! Dreams give us power!

Power to make changes in our life and the lives of others. Without power nothing will change.

If your true passion is a Ferrari, chase it with everything you've got, because when you get it, you'll not only have a Ferrari, you'll also have plenty of money to feed the poor.

Always chase your passion!!!

Chapter 7

Power of Pain
(Formula #2)

"The pain is not trying to stop you, it's trying to take you somewhere."

- Unknown

It was five years ago that Peter and Mary celebrated their tenth wedding anniversary. They had two beautiful children, a 6-year-old daughter named Anna and Thomas who just turned 5. Peter's background was in IT and his wife was an accounting clerk. They lived in a small townhouse and had 2 cars that worked, most of the time. For many years, Peter had struggled to hold onto a steady job. The IT industry had been hit hard and he'd only been able to get consulting contracts rather than full-time employment. The dry spells between contracts were always very financially challenging.

In this family, Peter was the one who handled the finances. Mary and Peter had a great relationship and Mary entrusted Peter fully to take charge of the family's money. Things were going pretty smoothly until they were hit with some unexpected financial obstacles.

One winter, after coming home from a beautiful holiday in Costa Rica, they found their basement completely flooded with 3 feet of water. Peter's DVDs and the kids toys were floating around in sewage. The stench was sickening. Peter was absolutely beside himself. Mary had never seen him so angry. She told him more than once, *"Peter, calm down. It's only water, the insurance company will take care of it."* As she said this, Peter's face immediately turned death white. He looked like he had seen a ghost.

Mary could not believe her ears as Peter began to tell her that he had not paid the house insurance premiums for the last 3 months because he was trying to catch up on some bills that were due. He was going to start paying the premiums again after the winter. The cost to repair the flood damage came close to $20,000.

The cost of the vacation was also put on credit card just like many other things. The card had been maxed out a number of times and Peter kept increasing the limit. He didn't want to disappoint his wife. He had to provide for his family and his dignity had to be upheld no matter what. The interest alone had reached almost $300 a month.

A week later, the transmission in one of the cars died. The car was not repairable and had to be replaced. To add to their misery, Peter couldn't find solid employment in his field so he had no choice but to take a full-time job in the shipping & receiving department of a paper company. It had a terrible work environment and paid half of his previous salary. Peter and Mary's financial situation was absolutely disastrous. Their savings account balance was virtually zero. The equity in their house was all used up to pay for the flood repair. The market value of the house was less than the mortgage they owed so they couldn't even sell it to get out of debt and their credit cards were maxed out. They were living and working just to pay the bills and some months they weren't even able to do that.

Peter and Mary's relationship had always been very good, but now the stress of their financial situation was pushing them to their limits of tolerance for each other. Even though Mary still respected and loved her husband, there was very little joy or patience left in their household. Every day as Mary came home from work, she would see Peter in his office with his head in his hands in complete despair. She didn't know what to say to him to get him out of his slump.

That was five years ago. Today, Peter and Mary's life is quite different. They have no debt and are very close to being financially independent. Mary work's part-time, only when she wants to. She loves being a full-time mom to her children; always there to welcome them when they come home from school... How did Peter and Mary's life change so drastically?

Peter had always been a dreamer when he was in his 20's. He wanted to achieve great success, but once he had a family, for some reason he started getting comfortable in his new world. He couldn't get the inspiration to just go and do what he always dreamt of doing. He kept feeling that he had to be home for his young children all the time. Somehow he lost sight of his dreams and started settling for whatever came his way. He just couldn't shake himself out of it. He was missing the catalyst, the spark that would reignite his inner fire.

For Peter, the catalyst was not his dream of great success, it was his pain. Let me take you back to a very special moment in Peter's life...

It was a cold wet Monday. The sun hadn't been seen for a while, it probably went on vacation. The sky was blanketed with dirty angry clouds. Peter had just finished work and was walking slowly towards his car in the parking lot. He was deliberately stepping in the puddles just to add some excitement to his monotonous life. He didn't care that it was miserable and cold. Even if it was a beautiful sunny day, he'd still feel miserable. It wasn't the weather outside, but the weather inside of Peter. He wasn't just tired from a hard day's work, he was mentally exhausted, drowning in debt and drained of all hope. It was as though he was living on the edge of a cliff on the verge of a mudslide.

When Peter finally got into his car, he didn't start the engine right away. Instead, he sat staring at the building that he just walked out of. The old worn out leather covering on the steering wheel began to slowly absorb the rain water on Peter's palms. The view through the windshield began to get misty as the heat from Peter's body rested on the cold glass, but Peter didn't need a clear view to see what he was looking at. For 10 long minutes, he sat piercingly starring at the building he worked at. His grip on the steering wheel began to get tighter and tighter. His face began to quiver a little. His eyes began to fill up with tears. One tear drop managed to escape his right eye and gently land on his lap. Peter brushed his eyes with the back of his hand and then started the engine. Before he drove off, he reached into his left inside jacket pocket and pulled out a CD that was given to him by a co-worker. He put the CD into the player, pressed play and drove off. He had absolutely no idea how much the decision to press play was going to affect the direction of his entire life forever.

The speaker on the CD was talking about the potential of the Network Marketing industry and about how anyone, from any background, could potentially become financially successful as long as they had a dream and a strong work ethic. The work ethic was key because they would be building a business outside of their full-time job. He then began to talk about success principles and financial freedom.

The CD finished just as Peter drove into his driveway, but Peter didn't exit the car. Instead he re-wound the CD to a particular part that he absolutely connected with...

"We all live in a country where we are free to make our own decisions on how to live our life. How many of you make decisions every day? You all have your hands up, but is this really true? Is it really YOU making those decisions? Let me ask you:

The time you set on your alarm clock to get up on a week day, is that your choice?

What you do for a living, is that your choice?

The number of hours you spend at your job, is that your choice?

The car you drive, is that your choice?

The amount of money you get paid from your job, is that your choice?

The amount of money that you give away to charities, is that your choice?

The meal you order at a restaurant, is that your choice?

The amount of time you spend with your children, is that your choice?

Where you go on vacation and how long you stay for, is that your choice?

When you're on your knees in the bathroom, reaching down into your toilet bowl to clean it with your own hands, is that your choice?

Let's not kid ourselves. We did not make these choices. It was the lack of money that made the choice for us. We may live in a free country, but the truth is, we are not truly free until we are financially free."

Peter suddenly reached over to the CD player and pressed stop. He had heard enough. All of a sudden he clenched his right fist and with white knuckles, he bashed the center of the steering wheel and started bawling. He was so disgusted and angry at the reality of his life. He knew he was solely responsible for his situation. He felt like a complete and utter failure. The mental agony, the excruciating pain had reached the pinnacle. He was at the fork in the road of his life.

Numerous people have been in a similar situation to Peter. It all boils down to how you interpret and internalize the pain. Many have interpreted the unbearable pain of failure, as a sign of the end of their journey. They allow the pain to destroy their hopes and dreams for good and simply give up. However, there are many great examples of successful people all over the world, who interpreted their pain completely differently. They chose to use the pain they were feeling to empower themselves. This is exactly what Peter chose to do also.

When Peter bashed his fist on the steering wheel, even though he was totally unaware, his pain was being internalized and transformed into power as he screamed the reality of his life into his mind...

"I hate my life!
I can't stand being broke!
Every time my kids ask me for something, I feel ashamed not being able to get it for them!
I hate my job, they treat me like a dog!
I am not going to live like this anymore!
Whatever it takes, I'm doing it... I'm changing my life!!!"

When Peter's pain level had reached the tipping point, it became the catalyst he desperately needed; a spark that ignited explosively within him and literally forced the direction of his life to shift dramatically through his attitude.

There is nothing wrong with allowing yourself to be inspired into action by your pain. Thinking about your pain is okay, as long as it's for a short period of time only. However, it will become a problem if you dwell on it, because what you *think* about, *speak* about and *feel* about continuously, you will attract more of it. So don't keep thinking about your pain. Use it only as a source of power to get yourself up and moving, then focus on the good you want in your life, rather than the bad you don't want.

Chapter 8

Power of Revenge
(Formula #3)

"The best revenge is massive success."

- Frank Sinatra

In the beginning of the movie 'Braveheart,' William Wallace was depicted as being comfortable living his life under the English tyranny. He was not inspired to fight it in any way at all. He just wanted to live his life as a farmer. Thereafter, a couple of his fellow Scotsmen approached him to join their secret meetings where they would scheme on how to attack the English...

"Your father was a fighter and a patriot." ...
"I know who my father was. I came back home to raise crops and God willing a family. If I can live in peace I will."

As a young boy Wallace had witnessed much death, including that of his father and brother. And even though he was now a young man capable of joining the fight, his motivation to fight the English was non-existent.

However, everything changed when his wife was abducted and killed. All of a sudden, Wallace was completely taken over by the grief and agony of his wife's brutal murder. His pain birthed a very powerful form of inspiration, *revenge*. This was the catalyst that ignited the fight and eventually led the Scots to freedom.

Revenge may be looked upon as a negative motivation, but many times along the journey of success, we will cross paths with certain individuals who become more than just critics in our mind. They have crossed the line. These people have somehow wounded us spiritually. Like a dagger still protruding from our heart, their scorn pains us to the core.

Sometimes there is no dream that can provide as much empowerment as the dream of revenge. Not the type of revenge as to hurt someone physically, but a battle of opinions and social status.

There are many very successful entrepreneurs who were continually inspired along their journey by the ridicule from their associates and certain family members. They constantly reminded themselves not only of what was said about them behind their back, but what was arrogantly said to their face:

What have you ever done in your life to be proud of?!
You're never going to make it!
Face it, you're a loser and you'll always be a loser!
You're going to quit this, just like everything else you've ever started!
It's not going to work!
Why can't you think for yourself? You've been brain washed again!
Still driving that crappy rust-bucket of a car?
I thought you said you were going to be rich?
I wouldn't date you, you've got nothing I want!
You can't even talk properly, you'll never be successful!
Who's ever going to hire you?
One in a million make it in that, you've got no chance!

Painful words such as these, with the right mind-set, can become very powerful sources of inspiration. And if we believe wholeheartedly, that the best revenge is massive success, we will be empowered to get up and continue to chase our dream until it is achieved.

Chapter 9

Power of Consequence

(Formula #4)

*"There are in nature neither rewards nor punishments,
there are only consequences."*

                   - Robert G. Ingersoll

It's 2:00am on a Thursday night. John just got in from a friend's 30th birthday party. He had an amazing time, but now he knows he's got to get to bed fast. As his head hits the pillow, he begins to dread the fact that in less than four hours, he has to get up and go to work. John's absolutely exhausted and falls asleep within seconds.

Just like every other weekday, the alarm clock starts buzzing loudly at 6:00am. John rolls over and instead of getting out of bed, he decides to sacrifice his breakfast cereal by hitting the snooze button. It got him an extra ten more minutes of sleep.

The alarm clock starts buzzing again. It seems to be even louder than before. John's head feels like it weighs a hundred pounds. He can barely lift it. It's as if the force of the deep sleep cycle is pulling him in. His mind begins to give his body a pep talk... *"You've got to get up, man! You have to go to work!"* ... *"I know, arghhhh!"* John reaches over and slams the snooze button again, this time sacrificing his shower for another 10 minutes of sleep.

The alarm clock goes off for a third time. John is in absolute sleep agony. He does not want to get up. All of a sudden he fully opens his eyes and stares into nothing for 5 long seconds. He then jumps out of bed, quickly gets dressed and rushes off to work.

What was John thinking when he was staring into nothing for the 5 long seconds? It was the very thing that got him out of bed... the consequences! As John lay in bed contemplating whether or not he should go to work that day, he started thinking about the consequences of sleeping in...

59

"If I don't go to work I'm going to lose my job... If I lose my job, I lose my pay cheque... If I lose my pay cheque I'm going to lose my car and my house... I'm going to work!" The power of the consequences empowered John to act accordingly and just like John, many times in our life the power that we need will not come from our dream, but from fear of the consequences: *"If I don't pick up that phone, I'm going to be a slave to money for the rest of my life!... If I don't do what needs to be done, I'm never going to be financially free!... If I don't talk to that girl, she's going to end up as someone else's wife!... If I don't chase my passion, I'm going to regret it for the rest of my life!"*

A few years ago when my older son was 17, he came and told me that he had made the decision to not go to university. Not only was I disappointed, but I was completely shocked because I had no idea where this was coming from. How could I possibly persuade him to go to university when I never went myself? He was doing exactly what I did when I was his age and now I know how my parents must have felt. Once I was over the initial shock of the news, I had an idea. I didn't fight him on his decision, instead I grabbed a couple of newspapers.

"Okay, let's assume you've finished school right now and you want to get a job. Let's look in the newspaper and see which jobs you would qualify for, considering you have no other job experience besides McDonald's and no degree." I began to read through the job listings that did not require a degree or any specialized education. As I read them out loud he replied with a *"Yes"* or a *"No"* depending on whether he would want this kind of job for himself:

"Courier driver?" – "NO"
"Warehouse worker?" – "NO"
"Factory worker?" – "NO"
"Retail sales clerk?" – "NO"
"Construction worker?" – "NO"
"Telemarketer?" – "NO"
"Gas station attendant?" – "NO"
"Waiter?" – "NO"
"Cleaner?" –"NO"
"Nanny?" – "NO"

"That's enough Dad, what about all the other good jobs?"... "Are you

talking about these career jobs?" I pointed to the management career opportunity job listings. *"Yes, those are the ones!"* I began to read out these job openings as well, and every one of them required either a degree or a degree and a minimum of two years of work experience. After he heard me read out about five of the job listings, he said exactly what I was hoping he would say, *"Okay Dad, I get your point!"*

The consequences of not having a degree motivated my son enough to get back on track with his studies and focus on getting into university. He qualified with an 88.8% average and got into the 'Business Management Co-op Program' at the University of Toronto. I didn't fight or push my son into making a decision for me. Instead, I got him to use his own imagination and go into his future to see what the consequences would be if he chose not to go to university. Once he experienced those consequences, he realized for himself that he needed to prepare more if he wanted a better future.

There is a scene in the movie 'Braveheart' where William Wallace is about to get on his horse and ride off to the talk to the Scottish Noblemen about joining forces in order to defeat the English. Wallace's best friend is trying to persuade him not to go because he thinks the Noblemen are working with the English.

"It's a trap, are you blind?!... We've got to try. We can't do this alone. Joining the Nobles is the only hope for our people. You know what happens if we don't take that chance?... What?... Nothing!... I don't want to be a martyr!... Nor I, I want to live. I want a home and children, and peace. I've asked God for these things, but it's all for nothing if you don't have freedom... It's just a dream William!... Just a dream? What have we been doing all this time? We've lived that dream."

When Wallace heard his best friend say, *"I don't want to be a Martyr,"* he knew fear had entered into the heart of his fellow warrior. Even though Wallace himself had fear of being captured, he was empowered by a greater fear of the consequences of doing nothing. Wallace knew too well that someone had to pay the price for freedom... and he was prepared to be that someone.

Are **YOU** willing to pay the price to change your life?

Chapter 10

Power of Accountability
(Formula #5)

*"I'm the only one that can be held accountable
for the way my life turns out. "*

         - Colleen Hoover

When the cat is away the mice will play! How do most employees behave after they find out their boss is going to be away for the day? It's quite humorous... some employees will go into their boss's office and sit on their chair with their feet up on the desk. Some will go for an extra long lunch and others will slack off completely and spend all day talking on the phone or surfing the net.

However, some people will tell you that their productivity is not affected at all by their boss's absence and that they will continue to work just as hard. I'm sure this is true for some, but for most employees, when their boss is not present their focus and productivity will definitely drop.

It is very tempting for entrepreneurs who are building their own businesses to slack off since they are the only person in charge. Many of them secretly wish they had a boss that they were accountable to because they know that if they had someone to report to, they would be more productive. At certain times in our life, being accountable to someone will actually empower us more than our own dreams. We will always go that extra mile and do more for someone else than for ourselves.

Jill was a Network Marketing entrepreneur and a single mother of two teenagers. She had been trying to build her business for quite some time. She had great talent and huge potential to become a big leader. She was not afraid to contact people and tell them about her business and she was also great at making presentations to groups of people.

Jill's number one challenge had always been consistency. She would be super active for a few days and then get distracted with life. Jill had big dreams for her and her children, but for some reason her dreams were just not powerful enough to keep her consistent.

Two years later, Jill achieved a very significant level in her business. During an interview on stage about her achievement, she was asked this very important question, *"What was the catalyst that created the momentum in your business?"* ... Here's her answer:

"My up-line leaders are Mary and John. Not only do I respect and admire them for what they have achieved in their business, but I truly respect them for the people they are. They are wonderful caring people of the highest integrity and character. Everything changed in my business when Mary called me and offered to be my accountability partner. It was a simple idea and yet so very powerful.

Each Sunday I would call Mary's voice-mail and tell her what my activity goal was going to be for the week. I would also give her a breakdown of exactly how I was going to achieve that goal. The following Sunday I would call her voice-mail again and report to her whether or not I had achieved my goal.

I had so much respect and admiration for Mary that I forced myself to perform. There was no way that I was going to break my word. I wanted to gain her respect and I knew the only way it would happen, was if I kept my word and did what I said I was going to do. The fear of losing Mary's respect empowered me so much that I did whatever I had to, in order to achieve my weekly goals.

The biggest challenge I struggled with at the beginning of this accountability program was that I kept thinking that Mary was too busy. She had so many people in her network, how could she possibly have time for me? I only started the program after she got my thinking straight by asking me two very important questions:"

"Jill, if 10 people in your down-line network asked you to be their accountability partner so they could report their goals and activity to you every Sunday, would you say you are too busy? ... Absolutely not! If I had 10

63

people reporting to me I'd be very excited... Why?... Because I'm looking for serious players to work with and this would show me who they were... Right! It's the same for me Jill, I'm looking to see who my serious players are also."

"If Mary hadn't called me that day I would still be struggling with my business. Thank God she did. Today, my business is exploding because I offered the same accountability program to my down-line team members and I have a lot of people reporting to me every Sunday. I love it!"

Chapter 11

Power of a Cause
(Formula #6)

"A man without a cause is nothing. He has nothing to look forward to, he has nothing to work toward; he is as a man lost, wandering in the darkest part of his heart to find a deeper, better purpose in his life."

- Hazel B. West

The movie 'Schindler's List' is about a man named Oskar Schindler, a German businessman and war profiteer. Oskar loved fancy clothes, wine, socializing and any opportunity to create wealth. Making money was always at the forefront of his mind. At the time of the Second World War, Oskar owned a factory that made pots & pans. When the war broke out, he was told by the Nazis that he needed to make ammunition otherwise they would close down his factory. He reluctantly agreed and then hired hundreds of Jewish employees to work in his factory only because they were the cheapest to hire.

As the war progressed, the Nazi officers gave orders to execute Jews everywhere. They were taken to the gas chambers by the thousands. The dead bodies were thrown into mass graves or burned. Oskar realized that the only Jews that were safe, were the ones that worked for him. His factory became a safe haven for Jews because they were making ammunition for the Nazis. The Jews who worked for him also realized, *"If you want to live, work for Oskar."* In an attempt to save more lives, many of Oskar's employees would recommend new potential employees for Oskar to hire; they were all family members.

Oskar began to realize that the Jews in his factory were only alive because of him. His conscience was screaming at him, *"You must do more Oskar! You must save as many lives as you can!"* Oskar took money out of his business and started to bribe the Nazi officers. He paid them money in exchange for more Jews to work at his factory. As he saw that the bribes were working, he made more bribes. His heart felt like it weighed a thousand pounds, ready to explode because he was racing against death.

Death was all around him. He kept taking more and more money out of his business to buy more Jews. At some point Oskar realized that the money he was blessed with, had only one purpose, to save lives. Oskar literally bankrupted himself by giving away close to four million dollars in bribes to the Nazis to buy and save over 1100 Jews.

When the war came to an end, Oskar Schindler had to flea because he was also a registered member of the Nazi Party. As he was exiting his factory, he was greeted by his accountant and one other man who presented some special papers to him. *"We have written a letter trying to explain what you did for us, in case you were captured. Every worker has signed it."* All 1100 people that Oskar saved had signed and confirmed the validity of the letter. This was 'Schindler's List.'

Oskar's accountant then stepped forward and presented Oskar with a gift. It was a solid gold ring. The gold had come from the teeth fillings of some of the men. They wanted to give something back to Oskar in gratitude for saving their lives. On the ring were engraved the words from the Talmud, *"Whoever Saves One Life, Saves The World Entire."*

The dialogue below reveals the new heart of Oskar Schindler. This man who was at one time only interested and motivated by money, somehow, amongst all the death and ugliness of war, discovered deep down inside of himself his true passion... his cause; to use his money and unique negotiation skills to save the lives of hundreds of people. As Oskar looked upon the gold ring in his hand, he whispered to his accountant...

"I could have got more out. I could have got more ... Oskar there are 1100 people who are alive because of you, look at them ... If I had made more money, I threw away so much money. You have no idea. If I had just ... There will be generations because of what you did ... I didn't do enough! ... You did so much ... This car, why did I keep the car? 10 people right there. 10 people. 10 more people! This pin, 2 people. This is gold, 2 more people. It would have given me 2 more, at least 1. It would have given me 1. 1 more. 1 more person Stern... For this!" Oskar fell to his knees, broke down in tears and cried out... *"I could have saved one more person and I didn't!"*

There will be countless people who will watch this movie and be completely captured and heartbroken by the pain and sorrow of such ugliness in the world, and yet at the same time, many others will be overwhelmingly empowered by the hope and inspiration demonstrated by Oskar Schindler. Many people, deep down in their hearts, will feel that they are just like Oskar. They have a burning desire to make a difference in the world and they too have realized that their true passion is a *cause*.

If you are inspired by a cause and really feel that it's your calling, your true passion, then put up a picture of *the pain* that you want to relieve. It's easy to say, *"I want to make a difference in the world"* and then do nothing. If we can't feel or see the pain in front of our eyes, we will lose the perspective and the power to make a difference.

If you want to help the poor starving children of the world, get a picture of a child in that very environment. A child who has no parents, no food, is diseased, drinking dirty mud water, with tears streaming down their lonely face. Put this picture next to your phone in your office. If you truly have a passion to make a difference in the lives of starving children like you say, each and every time you walk into your office, the face of this child will empower you to do something great with your life; to be that difference in the world.

There are many people out in society who are quick to judge those who have a lot of money or have the ambition to make a lot of money. They make ignorant comments like, *"Making money is a sin"* or *"Rich people are going to hell."* Unfortunately, the reality of this world is that people who have little money can do very little to help others. To change this world, it's going to take 2 things: money and *leaders* with the right heart. I did not say *people* with the right heart. There are a myriad of people with the right heart and no courage. Leaders with the right heart will make things happen even if they themselves have no money.

If you have the right heart and you want to make a difference in this world, go ahead and make as much money as you possibly can. This world needs more good people with lots of money... the more money you have, the more good you can do.

Chapter 12

Power of a Hero
(Formula #7)

"The hero is one who kindles a great light in the world, who sets up blazing torches in the dark streets of life for men to see by."

- Felix Adler

Your hero could be your father, your mother, a grandparent, a teacher, a celebrity, a saint or the founder of a religion. Your hero could even be Superman or Batman, because your hero... is *your* hero. Why do people admire heroes? It's not just because of what they've accomplished. People admire heroes because of the journey they've travelled. The things they went through, the struggles and the pain they willingly endured. And even when the odds were against them, they still had the courage to keep on fighting and never quitting no matter what. We admire heroes because of their willingness to sacrifice themselves for their cause.

A few years ago, all over my office walls I had pictures of beautiful mansions, Porches, Lamborghinis, Ferraris and vacation spots from around the world. I had scrapbooks full of pictures of dreams, and yet for some reason they all eventually lost their power to inspire me. I was completely devastated. How many more pictures of dreams do I have to get? It wasn't working and I couldn't understand why. Why wasn't I getting any power from these dreams? What's wrong with me?!

Unexpectedly, from one of the books I was reading, the author casually mentioned the word *hero*, and all of a sudden my whole perspective changed. I started asking myself, *"Who would I consider as being my hero?"* Over the next few days, I took down all the pictures that were on my office walls and put up pictures of my heroes.

At the top left of my office wall there is a picture of Harriet Tubman with a gun in her hand. She was born into slavery but after she escaped and got her freedom, she went back risking her life and her freedom 13 different times to free the other slaves.

Next to her, is a picture of Martin Luther King, Jr., with his hand raised as he was delivering the speech, 'I have a dream.' He risked his life for his cause every single day. Martin Luther King, Jr. was killed for sharing his dream with the world.

Next to him, is a picture of Mahatma Gandhi in his jail cell holding onto the prison bars. He put his life on the line in order to win independence for his country, India. After he succeeded, he risked his life again trying to keep the peace in his divided country. He was eventually assassinated.

Next to him, is a picture of Jesus from the movie, 'The Passion of The Christ.' He's not dressed in a three piece suit. He's holding onto the cross, with blood dripping down his face.

Beside him, is William Wallace from the movie 'Braveheart,' tied down and ready to be executed.

And finally there is Maximus Decimus Meridius from the movie 'Gladiator,' collapsed on the ground next to the graves of his murdered wife and son.

Above the pictures of my heroes I have a sign that says, *"Tired, Discouraged, Betrayed, Persecuted, Heartbroken... yet they would not give up!"*

When your children are hurting, do you hurt?... Do you feel their pain? When your parents are hurting, do you hurt?... Do you feel their pain? Of course you do! You hurt when they hurt. You feel what they feel, because of the love you have for them. Your hearts are connected so their pain becomes your pain. When you have a hero that you love and admire so much, you can feel their pain.

One of my heroes is Jesus. In the movie 'The Passion of the Christ,' I saw what they did to him. They spat in his face! They beat him! They whipped him! He fell to his knees and they kept on whipping him! But somehow, deep down inside of him, he was able to get the power to get himself back up even as they whipped him. All that pain!... and he took it! When life knocks me down and I feel great pain, I think of my hero's pain. His pain was so great. My pain is insignificant and nothing compared to his pain. I feel ashamed to stay down and think that life is too tough. His pain gives me the power to get myself back up... *"I am not staying down! I'm getting up, just like my hero did!"*

I meet a lot parents who tell me they want to be heroes to their family, but they are afraid. Afraid of rejection and ridicule. Afraid of what people may think of them as they attempt to build their business or share their passion. In the movie 'Braveheart,' there is a scene where William Wallace is in his prison cell, just moments before his execution. He drops to his knees and prays, *"Father, I am so afraid. Please give me the strength to die well."*

It's okay to be afraid. All heroes had fear, but they didn't let the fear stop them. Somehow, they pulled out power from within to overcome and conquer their fear. You have to ask yourself, *"Do you want to be a hero to your family?"* If you do, then you have to accept the fear and pull the power out from within your heart to overcome it, just like your hero did!

The Day My Father Became My Hero

I remember back when I was 14-years-old and living in England, my father owned a number of houses and retail stores. On this one particular day, he asked me if I would like to go with him to one of his suppliers to buy some merchandise to sell in the store. I agreed to go.

At the wholesaler's store, my father picked out what he wanted to buy and proceeded to the cashier. Once the invoice was ready, the cashier told my father the amount owing. My father pulled out his cheque book and handed it over to the man to fill out. I was a little confused as to why my father didn't just write the cheque himself and give it to the man. The man filled out the cheque and gave it back to my father. My father looked it over, signed the bottom and gave the cheque back to the man. When we got back in the car, I asked my father why he handed the cheque book to the cashier instead of writing the cheque out himself. I couldn't believe the answer he gave me... *"Because I can't read or write English."*

Oh, my, God! My father fooled everyone! We were living in England. Everyone spoke English. He achieved all this success and no one even knew he couldn't read or write English. That was the day my father became a hero of mine. My father didn't care that he couldn't read or write English, he had a dream and he chased it. He made no excuses. He did whatever he had to, to provide for his family.

The Tragedy of a Hero

When my father was 72, he was walking his grandchildren to school. On the way back home he fainted and fell to the ground. As soon as he regained consciousness, he got up and made his way back home. When he entered the house, it was obvious that something had happened. He had a cut on his forehead and a half-dried blood stain on his shirt. When I asked him what happened, he told me he didn't know.

It took two years and many tests for the doctors to finally figure out what was wrong with him. The neurologist told me that my father had a brain disease called PSP, *Progressive Supra Nuclear Palsy*. At that time, 1 in a million people were believed to have the disease. Today it is 1 in every 100,000. There is still no cure and no one has ever lived beyond 10 years after being diagnosed with the disease.

My father was a strong man, but after two years with this disease, I watched his health steadily deteriorate every single day, right in front of my eyes. The first significant thing that happened to him was that he couldn't keep his balance. Whenever he tried to walk by himself without holding onto something, he would lose his balance and fall to the ground. Sometimes, even if he was just standing still, he would suddenly fall backwards. This was a common symptom of the disease. He had strength in his legs but his nervous system couldn't maintain his balance.

In order to help my father exercise, while he was seated, I would get him to put his hands on my shoulders as I faced him, then I would pull his arms forward slightly, so most of his body weight was on his knees. He was then able to get himself up from his chair using the strength in his legs. Once he was standing, I would hold onto the sides of his arms to keep him balanced and begin to walk backwards. As I walked backwards, he was able to walk forwards without losing his balance. We would do this together 2 to 3 times every day.

This disease is such that it fools the person who has it in making them think they are completely fine to get up and move around. There were many times when my father would get up in the middle of the night and attempt to walk to the bathroom by himself. As I lay asleep upstairs I would be awoken by a loud bang! Immediately I would jump out of bed, sprint downstairs and find my father laying on the floor facedown and helpless. After helping him get back into his bed, I would walk back upstairs slowly, while listening out for any bit of noise indicating that he might be trying to get up again.

The first time this happened, I was completely speechless. The second time he did it, I was so angry at him. The third time, I didn't say much, because I realized he wasn't doing it on purpose, it was the disease. On the inside, my heart was being torn into pieces. I wanted to cry out loud, but on the outside, I had to maintain my composure in front of my mother, wife and children.

It was virtually impossible for me to sleep in peace knowing that my father would repeatedly try to get up again, so I purchased a small motion detector alarm that I placed on the floor. Anytime his feet came over the side of the bed, the alarm would ring. It worked great. I would joke with him that I had finally figured out how to catch him at his own game of trying to leave the room without being detected. His only response was a smile.

I had to install grab bars all over the area of the house that my father frequented to allow him to hold onto something while he made his way across the room. It worked great for quite a while because he didn't have to depend on anyone else in order to get up and walk across the room.

On this one particular day, I helped my father go to the bathroom. As he sat on the toilet I told him to tell me when he was finished so I could come back and help him get up. After a few minutes I heard a loud bang! He tried to get up by himself again and fell. And to make things worse, when he fell, he fell in front of the door, closing it shut. When I heard the bang, I ran to the bathroom but I couldn't get in. His body was up against the door. I had no idea whether he was having a heart attack or just fell again. Eventually I was able to get the door open, but that was not a good day. It was definitely what they call a *character building* moment.

Once again I had to come up with a solution to prevent him from falling off the toilet. I was able to get a wheelchair that could be wheeled right over the toilet. The chair had a seat belt which kept him safely secured upright. Not only did it help him, but it gave me a tremendous amount of peace knowing that he was safe. I also tied a small bell to the chair, so my father could ring it to let me know that he was finished. It could be heard from any room in the house. To this day, I can still here echoes of that bell ringing in my head. As the disease progressed, my father would have the occasional fainting spell while lying flat on his recliner chair. I could tell that he had fainted because his head was cold and dripping with sweat as he lay there panting. Besides raising his legs and lowering his head, there was nothing we could do except wait for him to wake up.

On this one particular day, we were headed to the doctor's office. I was helping my father walk down the front steps of the house and just as he got off the last step and onto the ground floor, he fainted in my arms in the driveway right beside the car. This was not the first time he had fainted so I knew exactly what to do, however, it was the first time it happened in the driveway. Luckily it was a warm summer day. He was on the ground for almost 20 minutes before I could get him up and in the house again. That was the last time he was able to walk down the front stairs to exit the house. From then on we had to get a stair lift installed to get him to the ground floor through the basement and exit in a wheelchair. The wheelchair became his only way of mobility. He was now getting more and more tired after walking only a couple of steps.

The next thing I noticed about my father was that he couldn't move his eyes properly. In order to focus on something he had to move his neck and head to get his eyes on target. Then his neck muscles began to get tighter and tighter. The only way he could focus on something on his left or right side, was to turn his whole body in that direction. Eventually he didn't even bother. It was too difficult for him, so he would simply try to rely on his peripheral vision.

The next thing to go was his speech. He started to slur his words. It was getting more and more difficult to understand what he was saying. It got so bad that I had to create a picture board of things for him to point at, in order for him to communicate what he wanted. That didn't last long either though, because he eventually started to lose the coordination in his hands to be able to point accurately. Then he lost the ability to feed himself. The only thing he could do well was to put his thumb up for a *"Yes"* and down for a *"No."* Those became his signature moves.

By this point, personal care workers would come to assist us in taking care of my father 2 to 3 times a day for an hour or so. They would help feed and shower him, but when they were gone it was all up to me. My Mom did so much for my father, but she was also in her late 70's and not capable of doing any of the physical work. My wife and two teenage sons were also a great help whenever they were available. Thank God I was financially free to be able to be there for my father 24 hours a day, 7 days a week.

When the personal care workers were not present and my mother was too tired, I had to feed my father. I had to clean his teeth. I had to shave him. I had to clean his ears. I had to clean his nose. I had to take him to the toilet. I had to shower him. I had to dress him. I had to exercise him... every single day. All of a sudden, reality hit me like a ton of bricks. My father's whole life was in *my* hands. He couldn't do anything for himself, he depended on me 100% of the time for everything.

My father, a strong and proud independent man, was trapped inside his own body. His mind was still working well, but his body became a prison. I remember this one day when some family relatives came to visit. As they shook hands with my father, he tried very hard to say something but couldn't get any words out. As they sat down, I saw the tears run down my father's face. He was so sad that he couldn't even greet his visitors properly. It was absolutely heartbreaking.

The next thing to go was my father's ability to swallow. People with PSP usually die as a result of swallowing difficulties. The inability to clear their throat results in fluids being inhaled into the lungs. My father started to eat less and less food because he was getting tired of trying to swallow without choking on his food. I could see the frustration on his face. The day I saw my father cough his guts out after he tried to drink regular water broke my heart. I knew things were progressing quickly down an unfortunate road.

Many times I would pray to God angrily, *"Why are you doing this to my father?!... How many more years?!... Five years!... Six years!... This is not fair! Why are you putting him through so much pain?"*

I couldn't comprehend or accept why this was happening to my father. I would hear about *bad* people who would get a heart attack and just die, but where's the suffering in that? Where's the pain?... And then you see good people like my father who was suffering for years. This is not fair. Why is this happening?

I prayed to God, *"I want my father to die!... Take him!... This is not right!... It's been seven years!... Why are you doing this?"*

Finally I got my answer. *"Many great people in history suffered, not because they did something wrong themselves, but they suffered to benefit others. Your father is suffering for you. I am giving you the opportunity to become a better son through your father's suffering. Serve him. When you become that son, I will take him."*

My father had six children. Five of them were perfect and one was an idiot. That idiot was me. Growing up, I argued with him constantly. I didn't even like my father most of the time and now, all of a sudden, I'm the one who has to look after him and become a better son. I don't even know how to become a better son and yet, according to the answer I got in my prayers, the length of my father's suffering was in my hands.

In my prayers, I asked God, *"When my Father dies, I have 2 requests: I want to be the first one who finds him. Not my mother or my wife or my sons. I want to find him first. And the second request is, I want my father to die peacefully.* " I knew this sickness was very bad. People who have this sickness do not die in peace, they choke to death. Those were my two requests to God.

For my father's sake, I now realized I had to become a better son. I had a lot of growing up to do because deep down I knew I was not a good son. I would easily get frustrated and sometimes even angry at my father when I tried to feed him. He would bite on the spoon and not let go of it. I thought he was doing it on purpose, but it was the disease that was causing him to lose control of his body. I guess the toll of always having to look after him was starting to show. Many times I just felt tired and trapped, always having to be there and not being free to just get up and go and do what I wanted to do. Even when we would go out to a relative's house with my father, it was not a relaxing time because I had to constantly be there to take him to the washroom two or three times and watch that he was okay and not about to fall off the sofa. I was getting so frustrated and worn out mentally because I couldn't relax my mind, there was always something that needed to be done 24 hours a day.

To keep my attitude in check and to empower myself to think and behave in a way that would serve my father, I created reminder cards. I read these cards every morning before I saw my dad. They would get me in the right frame of mind by reminding me how to behave in order to be the son my father needed me to be. This is what was written on the cards:

Papaji (Father)

"I never raised my voice... I never embarrassed him... I never insulted him when he was confused or slow to act... I never took advantage of his vulnerability... I respected him as my father... I was always there for him like he needed and wanted me to be... His quality of life was the only factor... Very soon he will be gone... Today, it may be the last time he can smile, say a word, move his legs, swallow, be able to put his thumb up, communicate or hug... Then there will be an empty bed... Just memories of his smile, laughter, vulnerability, helplessness and how I treated him."

A couple of years after my father was diagnosed with PSP, I noticed that his speech was getting a little slurred. I could still understand what he was saying but it was not as clear as it used to be. I decided to do some research about PSP and speech loss. All the experts said the same thing; my father was going to lose his speech as the disease progressed. Knowing this, I decided to make videos of my father. I asked him all sorts of questions about his life and recorded his responses. Questions such as: *"Why did you leave India and go to England?... What jobs & businesses have you had in your life?... What advice would you give to your great grandchildren about what is important in life?"*

As the disease progressed he spoke less and less. It got to the point where he hardly ever said a word. If we asked him a question, because he was trying to consciously tell us the answer using his brain and mouth, he just couldn't connect the two and get the words out. He had lost the ability to say what he wanted to say at the very moment he wanted to say it. We missed hearing his voice so much. How true the saying, *"You will only realize the value of something after you have lost it."*

However, occasionally at bedtime, as I entered my father's room unexpectedly and surprised him by saying, *"Goodnight!"*, his brain would somehow cause him to have an automatic response and he would reply back, *"Goodnight!"* The first time this happened, the whole family heard it and we all cheered like crazy. We started bouncing on his bed and kept hugging him. We were overjoyed to actually hear his voice again. He even smiled at our response. From that day on I kept a digital voice recorder close by. I was fortunate enough to capture a few more of his responses before they disappeared forever. These rare and precious little blessings would pop up and empower us amidst the pain and suffering of this long arduous journey that my father was on.

For my father, I would assume that one of the toughest parts, if not the toughest of his illness, was having to accept the hard inevitable reality that he could no longer shower or clean himself after going to the toilet. The most private and personal part of his life was about to become very public.

I remember the very first time I had to clean my father after he went to the toilet. I was filled both with nervousness and disgust. I was so uncomfortable with the reality of what I was about to do. The only way I could bolster up the courage to do it was to ignore how I was feeling and focus only on how I thought my father was most likely feeling. I needed to experience, if only for a moment, my father's *broken world* through his eyes. I needed to feel what he was feeling deep down in his heart. A heart that must have been wounded badly by the shame and despair of his illness. How is a proud man with great self respect, able to raise his head in dignity after being put in such a humbling, vulnerable and degrading position? Only an environment of pure love enabled my father to have the confidence to raise his head with dignity. He was completely protected and surrounded 24 hours a day by the love of his family.

As the disease progressed, my father had more and more difficulty with his swallowing. His weight was plummeting, he was simply getting too tired to eat. Even his drinking water had to be thickened first before he could attempt to drink it. The doctors advised us that a feeding tube should be inserted into my father's stomach, otherwise he wouldn't survive long on what he was managing to eat.

I remember the day he had the surgery at the hospital. After the procedure, we were told that he needed to stay in the hospital for a few days. On the first night, after all the other family members had gone home, I took a seat next to his bed. It was getting late, probably close to 10pm. The nurse came in and said it was best that I go home because there was nothing I could for my father while he was resting, and besides, there was only the one small chair to sit on. I told her it was okay and that I would rather stay with my father. There was absolutely no way that I was going to leave my father alone in a hospital.

Over the years, I had visited the emergency wards countless times. I had become a regular due to my elderly parents needing care. Most of the nurses I met were wonderful and caring people, but there was simply not enough of them. I witnessed so many elderly people left unattended for hours in the hallways of the hospital. It looked like their own children & family members had abandoned them. I used to wonder in disgust, *"Where are their children? Why are they not here? How can anyone leave their dependent elderly parents in someone else's hands? They should be ashamed of themselves!"*

Sitting in this small chair next to my father's bed was getting pretty uncomfortable. By now it was close to midnight and most of the lights in the ward were off. It was very quiet, so I got up, moved my chair to the side and without the nurses knowing, laid out my sleeping bag right on the hospital floor next to my father's bed. I used my coat for a pillow.

In the middle of the night, I heard my father moaning. Something was going on. As I got up, I noticed a tube hanging out from the side of his blanket. I moved the blanket to see what it was. To my horror, it was his feeding tube. He had pulled it right out of himself. I ran to get a nurse and as she rushed in to attend my father, she told me not to panic. *"This is quite common,"* she said. They had to repeat the surgery again the following day. Luckily, everything was okay the second time around and a few days later my father was able to go home.

Now that my father had a feeding tube, I had a lot of new things added to my daily routine. I had a written detailed schedule of everything I needed to do around the clock. I had to add: crushing the different pills he needed to take 4 times a day, connecting his feeding tube, injecting water into his stomach numerous times a day, turning him over in bed every 3 hours so he wouldn't get bed sores, massaging his legs so his muscles wouldn't atrophy and transporting him from the bedroom to the living room.

As things got more and more demanding with my father's needs, I had to continually empower myself with this mind-set, *"How can I say I love God and not serve my helpless father? My only proof that I truly love my Heavenly Father, is to serve and love my earthly father completely."*

On this one night I went down at 4:00am to turn my father over onto his other side. Once I did that, I noticed that he was trying to show me that his mouth was a little dry, so I got a sponge on a stick, soaked it in water and put it in his mouth. He didn't have his dentures in and so when he sucked on the sponge he looked like he was sucking a lollipop. I smiled at him, looked straight in his eyes and told him, *"You look so cute!"* I couldn't believe I said that to him. This was the same father who use to smack me on my ass when I was a child. And now I'm calling him cute. At that very moment I realized,

I had fallen in love with my father. During all those years of looking after him, my father never said a single bad word to me. How could I not fall in love with him?

At 7:00am the following morning I went to my father's room. As I was setting up his feeding tube I glanced down at his face. He was in the exact same position as I had left him in just a few hours earlier. For some reason I couldn't stop staring at his face. I noticed a puff of white moisture on the pillow next to his open mouth. My heart sank as the room filled with a deafening silence. In utter shock and dismay I came to that dreaded inevitable realization... my father had passed on.

Even though it was heartbreaking to loose my father, I was relieved for him that all the pain & suffering was finally over. He was no longer trapped in his body. He was permanently free. How wonderful he must have felt as he shed that old and worn out body of his after 81 years.

Only later that day did I realize, God had answered both of my prayers: I was the one who found my father first after he had passed on, and secondly, my father passed peacefully in his sleep... Thank you God!

When our children hurt, we hurt. When our parents hurt, we hurt. We can feel their pain because our hearts are connected. The pain and suffering my father endured for those 9 long years touched and changed my heart more than anything else in this world. The last year of my father's life was the greatest growing period of my life. As I served, sacrificed and loved my father, I truly believe our hearts became one. It was only after he died did I realize how much of a hero he really was to me. I look forward to that very special day in the distant future when I get the chance to once again hug my father and call him cute.

If you have an elderly parent or grandparent that is suffering and in need of care like my father was, please understand, you too have been given a great opportunity to grow and become a better son or daughter. I encourage you to serve and love them as best as you can. As you pour your love into their heart, God will pour his love into yours.

Chapter 13

Power of a Gladiator Statement

(Formula #8)

"I would like my life to be a statement of love and compassion, and where it isn't, that's where my work begins."

- Ram Dass

In the movie 'Gladiator' there is a scene where the emperor orders the Gladiator to remove his mask and show his face. *"Who are you?!"*

The Gladiator removes his mask and begins to speak... *"My name is Maximus Decimus Meridius, Commander of the armies of the North, General of the Felix Legion, loyal servant to the true emperor Marcus Aurelius, husband to a murdered wife, father to a murdered son and I will have my vengeance in this life or the next!"*

The Gladiator knew exactly who he was. His passion and purpose were burning inside of him like a fire that would not be put out.

Now, if someone asks YOU, *"Who are you?"* What will your answer be? *"I am a construction worker!... I am a doctor!... I am a lawyer!... I am a plumber!... I am an electrician!... I am a business person!"*

Is this who you really are?... Deep down in your heart, **who are you?!**

Many people hear negative thoughts in their head telling them constantly: *"You're good for nothing!... You're a loser!... You don't have any courage!... You've failed at everything in your life!... Nobody's going to respect you!... You're not going to make it!... Go ahead and quit, just like everything else you've always done in your life!"*

They hear these negative thoughts in their head every time they attempt to do something with their life. In the Bible it says that God *spoke* the world into existence. It doesn't say He *thought* the world into existence. Our voice

81

is louder than our thoughts. The negative thoughts in our head cannot be removed, but they can be drowned out by what we speak. We need to speak into existence who we want to be. Shout out loud your Gladiator Statement with power enough to drown each and every one of your negative thoughts:

"I'm a caring and understanding father!
I'm a loving and loyal husband!
I'm a respectful and responsible son!
I'm resilient! I'm focused! I'm disciplined! I'm a champion!
I'm a Winner!... I'm a Winner!... I'm a Winner!!!"

DROWN OUT THOSE NEGATIVE THOUGHTS!!!

Chapter 14

Power of Your 'Finest Hour'

(Formula #9)

"I believe a man's finest hour often comes when he is at his weakest.
When he is broken, affronted and at a place of great emotional transparency.
It's there he has the rare insight of an inescapable truth... he's merely a man.
As his bravado washes away into a puddle of reflective tears, it reveals that
he is merely flesh, blood and bones and amounts to very little without the
love and guidance of our creator. It's only then, that I believe,
a man begins to truly find his way."

- Jason Versey

In one of his most famous speeches, Winston Churchill spoke the following: *"The whole fury and might of the enemy must very soon be turned on us. Hitler knows that he will have to break us in this island or lose the war. If we can stand up to him, all of Europe may be free, and the life of the world may move forward into broad, sunlit uplands; but if we fail, then the whole world, including the United States and all that we have known and cared for, will sink into the abyss of a new dark age made more sinister, and perhaps more protracted, by the lights of a perverted science. Let us therefore brace ourselves to our duty and so bear ourselves that if the British Empire and its Commonwealth last for a thousand years, men will say, this was their finest hour."*

To paraphrase, back in the time of the Second World War, Churchill was telling the British people that Hitler was coming and many people were going to die, maybe even hundreds of thousands... *"Even though all the odds are against us and the whole world thinks that we don't stand a chance, we will not give in, we will not give up our freedom. We will fight anywhere and everywhere and a hundred years from today people all over the world will remember us and say, that was their finest hour; when all the odds were against them, yet they would not quit, would not give up their freedom... that is why they were victorious."*

I have spoken to thousands of entrepreneurs in business conventions all over the world and I know for a fact that at every convention there is always

83

a handful of people, who even though they are attending the convention, have already decided it was going to be their last one. They are only in the room because they had already purchased a ticket earlier on in the month. They have decided to quit because they can't take the pain anymore: the pain of fear, the pain of rejection, the pain of sacrifice, the pain of personal growth, the pain of being their own boss, the pain of no guarantee of success, the pain of ridicule from their friends & family, the pain of delayed gratification, the pain of struggle and the pain of trying to achieve their dreams. My friends, if you truly want to achieve your dreams, please understand you cannot do so without going through the pain. In this context, the pain is not a sign that you're on the wrong road, it's a sign telling you that you need to grow, to become better in all ways, in order to achieve your dreams.

When the pain of growth becomes almost unbearable and everything inside you is telling you to quit, you have arrived. Welcome to your 'Finest Hour.' Your finest hour will seem like the lowest point in your life. The only thing that will determine whether or not you will make it through your struggle will be your attitude. Anyone can have a positive attitude when life is good, but what separates the great people from the average is how they act when life knocks them down to their knees.

The movie 'Cinderella Man' is about a boxer named James Braddock and is set in the 1930s. It was the time of the Great Depression when 15 million people were unemployed. James would spend the day looking for work, usually at the docks loading the ships, and at night he would box whenever he could get a fight. He wasn't a good fighter, somehow he lacked the hunger even though he was totally broke. He had lost all his savings in the 1929 stock market crash. Even though things looked really bad for James, this was not his finest hour, it was going to get worse.

James lived together with his wife May and their three young children. One evening, as James was getting ready to leave for a fight, May told him that she got a final notice from the gas and electric company. The bills hadn't been paid and it was a warning that if they don't pay soon, the gas and electricity would be shut off. James told his wife everything would be okay, because he has another fight coming up soon and he'll be paid $50 whether he wins or loses. James then went to the front door to get the milk that should have been delivered by the milkman by now. When he got there, all he found were two empty milk bottles and a notice that said 'PAST DUE.' As he came back in, he showed May the notice and put it on the existing pile of bills waiting to be paid. May grabbed the milk bottle that had a little bit of milk remaining in it and added water to it. *"Who needs a cow?"* she said, as she filled her daughter's cup.

When James took a seat at the table to eat his dinner, his daughter Rosy asked her mom for some more ham. Her mother told her that she couldn't have any more because she was saving the rest for her brothers who were sleeping. James then began to tell his wife and daughter about a dream he had.

"You know May, I had a dream last night that I was having dinner at the Ritz with Mickey Rooney and George Raft. I dreamt that I had a steak. A thick juicy steak. Like this Rosy!... Then I had a mountain of mash potatoes and I went back for ice cream three times. I'm stuffed. I'm absolutely full and I cannot eat another thing. You want to give me a hand?" James then took his dinner, one small slice of ham, and put it on his daughter's plate. He then left home and headed to his boxing match on an empty stomach.

The next day James went to the docks to see if he could get some work loading the ships. He was one of dozens of men pushing themselves towards the front of the crowd with the hope of being chosen to work and make some money. He wasn't chosen. When he got back home that day, his daughter came running to him, *"Jay stole!"* Jay was her brother. He was the oldest of the siblings, probably about 10-years-old. He had stolen some salami meat from the butcher. James took his son back to the butcher's store and made him return what he had stolen. On the way back home Jay began to reveal to his dad why he stole the meat.

"Marty Johnson had to go away to Delaware to live with his uncle because his parents didn't have enough money for them to eat... Yeah, things ain't easy at the moment Jay, you're right. There's a lot of people worse off than we are and just because things ain't easy that doesn't give you the excuse to take what's not yours, does it? That's stealing, right? We don't steal. No

matter what happens, we don't steal, not ever. You got me?... Yes... Are you giving me your word?... Yes, I promise... And I promise you, we will never send you away!" Jay jumped into his father's arms in tears. It was the only place where he knew he was completely safe. This was still not James' finest hour, things were going to get worse.

That night James had a fight to go to. As he was getting ready in the locker room, his manager noticed that his hand was injured, it hurt every time he put pressure on it. *"Why didn't you tell me?"*, his manager complained. James whispered to him in desperation, *"I owe everybody money, I can't get any shifts, I ain't got any cash."* His manager sympathized with his situation and began to double tape his hand and wrist for extra protection. The fight that night turned out to be a disaster, James couldn't fight aggressively enough due to his broken hand and so the fight was classified as a no contest. Not only was he not paid but his license to fight in the ring was revoked, he was decommissioned.

When he got home that night, he told May what had happened and also that his hand was broken in three places. *"They said I'm through May, they said I can't be a boxer no more... Jimmy if you can't work, we ain't going to be able to pay the electric or the heat, and we're out of credit at the grocers, so I think we need to pack the kids. They could stay at my sister's for a little while and I'll take on more sewing. You can't work because your hand's broken."*

James explained to May that if he coloured his white plastered hand no one at the docks would notice that his hand was broken and he'd still be able to work when he got a shift. He grabbed the shoe polish and asked May to colour the plaster black. As May held his hand, James whispered to her, *"I'm sorry."* May could see the tears fill up in her husband's eyes, his heart was breaking under all the pressure. May loved her husband dearly, she didn't want to see even one teardrop fall from his eyes, so she got up and lovingly embraced him to ease the pain in his heart. However, this was still not James' finest hour, things were going to get worse still.

The next day James was lucky enough to get a shift at the dock. He made $6.74 after working all day, only to return home to a dark house. The electricity and gas had been shut off. To get it back on, he needed to pay $44.12. There was no way he could do it.

May lit candles and placed them all over the apartment and as they sat at the table, she offered her hands to her husband to pray. James placed his hands in hers, smiled and bowed his head. The room was so cold, their warm breath was completely visible as they breathed out in frustration. As May was about to speak, she was interrupted by their youngest son coughing in his sleep. When she told James that his cough started earlier that day, his smile turned into despair. James knew that if his son's cough got worse he'd be in big trouble. Where would he get the money to buy the medicine? May let out a sigh and then began to pray. While she was still praying, James raised his head and dropped his hands in disappointment. *"I'm all prayed out."* As May glanced at her husband, he looked down and shook his head in silence, as if to say, *"God's not listening."*

The next day, as James returned after working a shift, he walked into a quiet house. May was standing anxiously in the kitchen all alone. She began to explain...

"Owen's fever started to get worse and then Rosy started to sneeze."
James rushed into the children's bedrooms, only to discover empty beds.
"Where are they May?!"
"Jim, we can't even keep them warm!"
"Where are the kids?!"
"The boys are asleep on the sofa at my father's in Brooklyn, and Rosy will stay at my sister's. Jimmy we can't keep them!"
James started to shake his head in anger and defeat, *"You don't make decisions about our children without me!"*
"But what if they got really sick? We already owe Dr. MacDonald."
"If you send them away, then all of this has been for nothing!"
"It's just until we get back to even."
"What's it all for? If we can't stay together that means we lost, we've given up."
"I am not giving up! I am trying to protect our children!"
"May, I promised him! Outside the butcher's, I looked him in the eyes and I

promised him with all of my heart I would never ever send him away! You can't do this!"... "You weren't here."... "I can't break my promise!"... "Jim, you didn't see, you weren't here. I'm sorry! I'm sorry Jimmy!" James started emptying his pockets on the table. All he had was some change, then he headed for the front door. *"What are you doing, Jim?"* James looked at May in remorse for breaking his promise to his son. He shrugged his shoulders and stormed out of the house. Even though this situation was excruciatingly painful for James, it was still not his finest hour.

He headed straight to the emergency relief office and signed up for welfare. To James this was a sign of defeat, but he had no choice. He had to get his children back. The lady that served him, knew him well. *"I never thought I'd see you here Jim."* He walked away completely ashamed and embarrassed at his situation.

Even though he got some welfare money, it wasn't enough. So he headed to the lounge at Madison Square Garden where the members of the boxing commission hung out. As he walked the streets towards the building, it was as though he was about to be stripped of any self esteem and dignity that remained. Every step closer was like a dagger in his heart. He walked into the lounge. All the men knew him as James Braddock the failed boxer, the *has been.* He stood where they could all see him and the room went silent. James Braddock's finest hour had finally arrived. He had fallen to the lowest point in his life. He was completely broken and helpless...

"The thing is, I can't afford to... I can't afford to pay the heat. I had to farm out my kids. They keep cutting shifts down at the docks and you just don't get picked every day." James removed his hat and in complete humbleness began to beg. *"I sold everything I got that anyone would buy. I went on public assistance. I signed on at the relief office. They gave me $19. I need another $18.38 so I can pay the bill and get the kids back. You know me well enough to know that if I had anywhere else to go, I wouldn't be here. If you can help me through this time I would sure be grateful."*

Some of the men turned their face away in disgust, but enough chipped in to help James get his children back.

I truly believe that because James Braddock did not steal or go against his morals and lived up to his values, God took all the pain he went through and used it as a condition to bless his life greatly.

From that day on, James Braddock's life changed considerably. His hand eventually healed and he got another chance to fight in the ring again. But this time when he fought, it was totally different. He fought with great intensity and passion. He had a new dream. Every time he got hit, he envisioned the sign on the empty milk bottles, *"PAST DUE."* It gave him the power he needed to fight and win in the ring. He was never going back to that life again. **It seemed as though all the struggles he went through had come together to create the hunger he so desperately needed in order to change his life.** James Braddock eventually went on to become the Boxing Heavy Weight Champion of the World in 1935 and held the title for over 2 years.

If you are reading this book and thinking things are bad in your life, hang in there. Don't quit when you're down! Understand, no matter what you do in life, you can never avoid the pain of personal growth. I truly believe, just like it was with James Braddock, God will use the pain you are going through, as a condition to bless your life greatly, as long as you stay true to His values.

Chapter 15

Power of Your 'Invisible Friend'
(Formula #10)

"Never lose hope, my heart, miracles dwell in the invisible.
If the whole world turns against you keep your eyes on the friend."

- Rumi

The world is filled with lonely people; people who are struggling endlessly and have no one to talk to. From where does a person get the power to chase their dreams when they have so much hardship and misery in their life? When your heart is filled with pain and sorrow, how do you empty it?

I come from a culture that has an unspoken code of personal responsibility: *"If you're hurting, don't tell your wife. Don't tell your children. Don't tell your parents. Don't mention it to anyone. Keep it inside. Be a man and handle it yourself!"*... Sounds almost like an inspirational warrior creed.

There was a time in my life a number of years ago, when it seemed like everything was going wrong. My whole world was crumbling around me. I felt completely powerless, drifting amidst waves of endless years of disappointment and failure. My heart was aching with despair, longing to connect with someone or something that could ease the sorrow. I used to hear religious ministers on TV say, *"If you're feeling down, you need to pray."*... I tried that, it didn't work for me. When I prayed, it was like talking to a brick wall, I heard no answers. So I knew conventional prayer was not the solution for me.

Strangely, my mind took me back to a specific time in the past. It reminded me of a movie that I once saw when I was a child. This movie was about a little girl, probably 6-years-old, who lived with her parents. On this one particular day, as the girl's parents were sitting in the living room downstairs, they began to hear their daughter talking to someone in her bedroom upstairs. The parents whispered to each other, *"Who is she talking to?"* There was no one else in the house.

90

The girl's father quietly crept up the stairs and peeked into her room. He saw his daughter beautifully dressed sitting on a chair at a table laid out with 2 plates, 2 cups and a teapot. She was sitting across from an empty chair. Then all of a sudden, she began to talk to an invisible friend sitting on the other chair. *"Isn't it a beautiful day?... Would you like some tea?... I love your dress... Oh, you like my dress too?... This is such a wonderful day."*

The only thing I remember about this movie was the joy on this little girl's face as she talked to her invisible friend. She was so happy. I don't know what made me think of this movie or the girl, but I decided that day, to do the exact same thing. I decided to get myself an invisible friend that I could talk to. My invisible friend however, was going to be the greatest friend anyone could possibly have in the world. My invisible friend was going to love me so much, would always be willing to listen to me anytime I needed to talk, to support me always, to never judge me, to always forgive me and to always be there for me. I'm going to be able to tell my invisible friend anything & everything on my mind and in my heart.

Since I have the greatest invisible friend that anyone could possibly have, my friend needs to have the greatest name. What name am I going to give him?... I know!... There is no greater name than this. I'm going to call my invisible friend, 'God.'

I got myself a new journal to write in and just like a movie script I decided to record my conversation with my invisible friend. I wrote my name at the top left hand side of the first page and next to it, I began to write my conversation:

Terry - *"Hello God, how are you today?"*
Then as quickly as I could, I wrote a reply from my invisible friend,
God - *"Hello Terry, I'm doing good, how are you?"*
I stopped writing and whispered quietly to myself,
"This is crazy! What am I doing? If someone saw me doing this they would think I was nuts, just like that little girl!"

I kept picturing in my mind how happy that little girl was as she talked to her invisible friend. So I closed the door and continued to write.

"Hello God, are you really there?"
"Of course, I'm always here for you."

Again I stopped writing. I slammed the pen down on the table and shouted, *"What am I doing?! This is not God! This is me with a pen!"* I was in a battle with my thoughts... *"Are you nuts?! Why are you doing this?... I want to do this because I want to believe! I want to believe he's here! I want to believe he can hear me! I don't care what anybody else thinks! I want to believe!!!"*

I picked up my pen and continued the conversation. *"God, I'm feeling so down. My businesses have collapsed. I've lost all my money. I feel so embarrassed and ashamed. I have nothing left. My marriage is in a mess. I don't know what to do. I have no one to talk to. Can you help me?... Terry, it's okay. I'm here. Everything's going to be alright."*

I continued to write all that was on my mind. Every concern and worry that I had in my heart, I told my invisible friend. I kept writing and writing. For hours and hours. For days, weeks and months, I kept writing. I desperately wanted to empty my heart of all the pain that kept lingering on and simply would not go away.

As my relationship progressed, I began to ask my invisible friend questions. *"God, how should I treat my wife?"* Surprisingly the answer I got back was another question. *"How do you think you should treat your wife?... Well, I think I should treat my wife like this, and this, and this. Is this right?... Do you think it's right?"* I couldn't believe his answer. It seemed like my invisible friend was a master at sales. He would always answer my question with another question. But I continued to write.

After a few months, something unbelievable happened. My heart was completely empty of pain. I felt so light. I couldn't think of a thing that worried or concerned me. The sadness had completely gone. I felt like I had the greatest secret in the world. My invisible friend was with me everywhere I went. I didn't even need my journal. As I walked I would ask him, *"God are you there?"* And he would reply, *"Yes, right behind you."* I felt so empowered by the knowledge of his presence.

I encourage each and every one of the readers of this book to do the same. Even if you have someone close that you can talk to, I would still encourage you to talk to your *Invisible Friend*. Try it for 6 months, you'll be amazed. Inner peace, joy and empowerment are the fruits of this relationship.

Only years later would I realize how absolutely invaluable the discovery of my invisible friend was going to be to me.

Six months after my father passed away, I went to India to take his ashes to a holy site in his homeland. In India, two days before I was about to return to Canada, I was in my hotel room checking my emails. I quickly skimmed through most of them and suddenly stopped at this one email. As I began to read it, my heart sank into my stomach. The email was referring to an investment that I had made a few years earlier. It basically said that the owner of the company had embezzled the funds and the balance of the investment I had made of $125,000 was now $0. The money was all gone. My heart stopped beating. A cold sweat enveloped my whole body. I gently dropped to my knees clutching my stomach. I felt as though I was going to vomit. Even though I fought to hold them back, my eyes quickly filled with tears. I was simply devastated. I felt so embarrassed and utterly lost for words. Here I was laying my father's ashes to rest and now I have to deal with this humiliation.

There was nothing else I could do but talk to my invisible friend. As I was about to begin, my mind took me into the past. I began to recall a specific event 26 years ago, when I was given an audio cassette tape of a very wealthy man named Dexter Yager. On this tape he was talking about an investment he had recently made and was waiting to hear back about the outcome. He knew that something had gone wrong with the investment but didn't know all the facts. He was waiting for a confirmation of the loss. Upon receiving the update, he realized he had lost 80 to 90% of his wealth. He then proceeded to tell his wife, Birdie, that it was confirmed, they did lose the money. His next few words were what I remember as being totally profound. Here's the conversation between him and his wife as best as I can remember.

"Birdie, let's go!... Where are we going?... Dream-building!... Why would you go dream building Dex, when we just lost so much money?... We gotta dream bigger! The bigger the dream, the smaller this obstacle will look!" As I repeated Dexter's words in my head and then out loud to myself, I began to feel an overwhelming sense of empowerment. I got on my knees and started to pray. I asked God to lead me and show me how I can do even greater things with my life for him. Things that I could never even imagine. Things that are so big that will make this obstacle look like nothing. I told God that I totally believe in his direction and that I know he will open all the doors for me to accomplish these new, bigger goals and dreams. I felt so empowered after I prayed. I thought to myself confidently, *"God's going to open all the doors now, because I have shown him that I have faith!"*

Two months later, I was booked to speak at a convention in California. I headed to the Toronto airport and as I attempted to make my way through the United States immigration, I was stopped by the officer. The immigration officer told me that I needed a special Visa to enter as a professional speaker. I was completely ignorant about how a Visa worked and said to him, *"Okay, how much is it?... This is not how it works,"* he said. *"You need to leave the airport and apply for a Visa and then upon approval you can enter the U.S.... But I have hundreds of people waiting for me!... I'm sorry, there is nothing I can do. You have been refused entry for not having the right paperwork."*

I was completely devastated. Making the call to the California convention organizer and telling him that I was refused entry was the most embarrassing thing that had ever happened to me in my life. As I departed the airport, dejected and sick to my stomach, I felt as though I had been robbed at gunpoint. All the hope, all the dreams I had, were crushed with one blow. I couldn't believe what had just happened. I thought God was going to open up all the doors. It made no sense... why did God shut this door with such force?

On the following Monday morning I went to see an immigration lawyer. He told me that my situation was quite common and easily fixable for a fee of $1100. After talking to him I felt more relaxed and definitely found myself breathing a little easier. After I paid him the fee, he submitted all the necessary paperwork within a few days. A few weeks later he told me that I had been refused again and that the only thing to do next was to apply for a more complicated Visa. This other Visa was more expensive and harder to qualify for. It was the only other option remaining. The lawyer's fee alone was going to be $3500 with no guarantee of approval. I had no other choice but to start the process. The month was January.

In February I went to a shopping mall with my mother. Typically my mother and I would walk beside each other, but on this particular day for some reason she was walking a little faster than normal. I noticed something very strange as she went ahead of me. She seemed to be walking diagonally. I speeded up to her and as I said, *"Why are you walking like that?"* I was horrified to notice that one side of her face had dropped. I knew this was a sign of a stroke. I was scared to tell her what I could see because she was a worrier. Thank God the Doctor's office was literally 50 feet away from us. The Doctor told me to take her to the hospital immediately.

At the hospital the Doctor proceeded immediately with a brain scan. A few hours later, as my mother lay asleep, the doctor came back with the results. He told me that my mother had an inoperable brain tumour of the worst kind. She had about three to four months to live and there was nothing they could do. *"I'm sorry,"* he said.

I walked back behind the curtain to where my mother lay asleep in the emergency ward. As I looked down at her face peacefully sleeping, my heart broke. Tears began to run down my face. All my life I was always there for my mom. Always there to serve her. Always there to protect her, and now I was completely helpless. I couldn't do a thing to help her. I sat down on the chair beside her bed, took out a piece of paper and began to write to my invisible friend...

2:20am

"Good morning my dear Heavenly Father."
"My dear son, I understand what you are going through. I am here for you. You have cared for your parents so diligently. You make me proud to see you serve. My dear son, be strong and have faith. ALL is good. ALL will be

95

okay. I am here for you. I understand your pain, your anxiousness, your tears, your frustrations, your worry. It is okay my son, be strong, I am watching all. I am taking care of things in all directions. Please, my dear son have faith in whatever happens. I am here. All will be ok."

"Thank you so much Heavenly Father, I don't know what I would do without you. My heart would burst. Thank you so much. I can feel you in my heart, thank you. I need you today more than ever. If it be possible please let her tumour dissolve and disappear, but not as I wish it, but as Your Will be done. I love my mother so much, but I understand and love you also. I have complete faith that you will take care of my mother whether it's here on earth or in the spirit world. I would hope so much she can be with us longer and in good health... I leave it to you. But please understand, as you know already, I beg of you, a miracle in Jesus' name. Heavenly Father I totally understand if you take my mother, for I know too well that many young people have suffered the loss of both of their parents at a very early age in their life; the excruciating pain and heartache of not having parents. I suffered none of that. I had so many beautiful times serving and being loved by both of my parents. I was truly blessed. I know too well how you must have felt as you lost your son Jesus, how he was tortured, the heartache you went through, the sorrow. Your heart must have broken into so many pieces. I truly understand if you have to take my mother for whatever reason, just like Jesus had to leave the Earth, so who am I to beg you to save my mother and to give me more time with her? Who am I, but someone who loves you dearly and trusts you. Whatever Your Will is Father, I am in favour.

Heavenly Father, please guide my heart, mind and soul to serve my mother here and my father in the spirit world, to be continuous in my filial piety. Father please use me to love others with kindness of heart, words and actions. Please help me to love my mother more than I have ever done before. Please guide the doctors who are reviewing my mother's case to be inspired and touched by your heart and wisdom, to do what You desire to be done.

Heavenly Father I will begin a 24 hour fast from now. Please use this as a condition to heal my mother in any way possible, as long as it is Your Will.

Heavenly Father, I would like to give you a hug. You must hear the cries & prayers of so many that your heart constantly overflows with the heartache of your children. Heavenly Father, this son who is writing to you, praying to you, loves you dearly. I'm here to wipe the tears from your eyes, to put a smile on your face, to hold you, to give you back joy. I love you my dear Heavenly Father.

I understand your pain Heavenly Father, I am so sorry that so many have hurt you, over and over again. Please forgive them. I will do what I can to give you joy in their place. Heavenly Father please use me. Heavenly Father please forgive me for not being a better son to you earlier in life and a better son to my Earthly parents sooner, and a better father to my boys sooner, and a better husband to my dear wife sooner. I love them all so much. Please take control of my heart and help me to love them more.

Heavenly Father please help my brothers & sisters. Knowing about our mother's current situation will be heartbreaking. Please guide their hearts to know ALL will be well. Please guide my heart to love them all in this trying time.

Heavenly Father please don't worry about me, I'll be okay. I'll be strong. I am a soldier of Heaven, I will make you proud. I will work so hard to help spread kindness around the world. I will be caring, forgiving, compassionate and at the same time I will be a lion for You, in courage & heart, to do Your Will. Please guide me. I love You so much dear Heavenly Father."

Before I was refused entry into the U.S., I had speaking engagements booked on every weekend during the month of May. After I was refused entry I had to cancel all of them. My mother died three and half months after her tumour was discovered, on May 16. If I had not been refused entry I would have missed her passing. The day I got refused entry felt like one of the worst days I had ever experienced. How totally wrong I was, it actually turned out to be one of the greatest blessings of my life. Because of the refusal to enter the U.S., I was completely free to spend every day, 24 hours a day, at my mother's side. I got the chance to make all sorts of videos. Those videos and last memories with my mom were priceless. She hung in

97

for my birthday on May 11th. I was able to take a picture of me kissing my mother for the very last time on my birthday. Thank God I was refused entry. On May 16 my mother, as she was surrounded by so many loved ones, took her final breath. It was so final, and so excruciatingly painful as I realized what had just happened in front of my eyes. The one moment we were all dreading had just quietly come and gone. Everything was suddenly over. My mother's journey on Earth had ended. At that very moment the room burst out with cries of broken hearts and waves of tears as we all realized we would never get to hear her voice again. Our mother would never again comfort us in her arms. In order to take a breath, I slowly raised my head above the grief in the room and glanced out of the window. As I looked out at the trees gently swaying in the wind, I heard the comforting voice of my Invisible Friend, *"Everything's going to be alright."*

Only after my mother passed away did I truly realize the role she had played in my life:

My Mother, what did she ever do for me?
She wasn't there to prevent my struggles.
She wasn't there to prevent my pain.
She wasn't there to prevent my tears.
What did she ever do for me?
Every day when I awoke, she was there.
Every day when I came home, she was there.
Every day when I went to bed, she was there.
She was always there.
Even when so many times,
I never noticed her,
I never acknowledged her,
I never thought about her,
She was always there.
She was always there in the background of my life,
So I could one day, be on the center stage of mine.
She was always there.
My Mother, she was always there!

- Terry Gogna

My mom passed away exactly 1 year and 2 days after my father. Most of my family members looked at me as being one of the strongest in the family because I was a personal development coach and motivational speaker. They all believed I was handling my mother's death very well. They had the impression that I was emotionally strong and never got down.

A couple of weeks after my mom passed, I remember this one particular day. I went to the living room at the back of my house where my parents spent most of their time and as I sat on my father's recliner, I could see on my right, the cushions on the sofa that my mother would rest her head on in the afternoon sun. On my left, I could see my mother's little red slippers, eagerly waiting for her to take a walk. As I sat in the chair I couldn't help but think about my parents. I lived with my mother and father for 45 years and now they were suddenly both gone, within one year. The house was painfully quiet. I felt so alone.

My faith was being pushed to its limit. I no longer had the spiritual or emotional strength to hold back my tears. I completely broke down and cried out to God in utter sorrow... *"Why did You have to take both of my parents? It's not fair!"...* *"Why are you blaming Me for taking your parents? You should be thanking Me for giving you parents for 45 years!"*

My heart was completely broken and torn into a million pieces. I couldn't stop the tears. I loved my mother more than anyone else in the whole world and now she was gone. I missed her so much. All the formulas I had discovered over the years that I would speak about at conventions were completely powerless in this time of despair. I couldn't get myself up to do anything. I had lost the power to chase my dreams.

Suddenly, I heard a voice in my head, *"You speak to your Invisible Friend all the time, so why don't you speak to your mother? What would she say to you if you could hear her now?"*

I immediately grabbed a piece of paper and began to write. I wrote exactly what I was inspired to write from my heart; the words I believe my mother would say to me if I could only hear her voice...

99

A Message From 'Bibi' (Mother)

"Your Papaji (father) and I have not left you. We are frequently visiting you all at your homes. As having only a spirit body we can travel within seconds anywhere. We are free to travel from the spirit world to you anytime we choose because of your love for us. If you need us, all you have to do is call us in your thoughts and we will come to you in seconds. If all of a sudden you have feelings of sadness and start to miss us, it's because we have come to visit you. We both miss you all so much, but when we come to visit you, our presence is felt by your spirit and causes you to feel sadness in your heart. The sadness will eventually go away, it's just a part of life. When we visit you, we can see and hear everything you are doing in your homes. Even though you can't communicate with us at this time, it won't be this way forever.

When a person passes to the spirit world it becomes very heart breaking because you can no longer see them with your physical eyes. There is a reason for everything. When you lose a loved one, this is the only time you will be motivated to develop your spiritual senses. As you begin to pray more, you will start to feel and hear us deep down in your heart. We will be guiding you every day, so please try hard to listen. Please talk to us, we can hear everything you are saying. Tell us how you are feeling and what you are thinking about. Tell us about what is going on in your life. We are still here, we can hear you. I know it is hard, but please have faith that this is true.

Your Papaji & I are on a beautiful adventure together. We are visiting so many friends & relatives that we have not seen for a very long time. It is all very exciting and the best part is that it is all physically pain free. The spirit world is a beautiful place when you're loved. Your Papaji & I want you to live your lives fully, knowing that we are with you each and every day forever. You must be strong and build your families the way we did, with lots of love. We lost our parents too. Remember when the sadness comes on strong, it means we just walked into your home, so please don't cry, but talk to us. You know how much we both loved talking to everyone, especially me on the phone every day...We love you so much.

Your Bibi"

100

The most amazing thing happened after I wrote this letter. All the pain was suddenly gone. I didn't feel alone anymore. I wholeheartedly believed and still believe to this day, that these words came directly from my mother's heart.

This beautiful letter wiped away all the tears & sadness from my heart like only the comforting arms of a mother could do. It gave me the peace I so desperately needed. It was this peace that empowered me to get up and start chasing my dreams again.

I have spoken on many stages to thousands of people in numerous countries around the world and people ask me all the time, *"Don't you get nervous when you're on stage talking to so many people?"* I tell them all the same thing:

"I am always a little nervous, but never afraid because I am not here alone. There are four of us on this stage... Me, my Father, my Mother and my Invisible Friend."

Please understand, when you chase your passion with all your might, there will be many times along the journey where you will find yourself rejected and all alone. You're never alone! Your Invisible Friend is always right beside you, waiting for you to make the first move. All you have to do is have faith, reach out and talk to Him.

Chapter 16

Power of Love
(Formula #11)

*"You know you're in love when you can't fall asleep,
because reality is finally better than your dreams."*

- Dr Seuss

All throughout my teenage years I found myself struggling tremendously with a low self esteem, especially when it came to girls. I would always lack the courage to ask a girl out on a date. I was absolutely petrified of hearing a *"No."* But it wasn't the rejection that I was afraid of. What worried me the most was if she told her friends that she turned me down because I wasn't good enough for her. The fear of embarrassment held me hostage throughout my entire youth.

It was a cloudy summer's day in Birmingham, England. I was 16 and bored out of my mind. I was on my summer break and was standing beside the front door of my parent's shop looking out at the street. I wasn't looking at anything in particular, just passing time, hoping there might be something interesting going on outside to add a spark to all the monotony. All of a sudden my eyes were magnetized to a stunningly beautiful girl. She had long dark hair with bangs across her forehead and was wearing a Gypsy-type dress with thin straps. I was finding it difficult to catch my breath as my heart began to beat faster and faster. The longer I stared, the further away from me she was getting. *"What if I lose sight of her?"* I thought. I immediately opened the door and began to discretely follow her. She disappeared into a pharmacy. I crossed over the street and looked into the store. To my surprise, she was working behind the counter as a cashier. *"Yes!"* I quietly whispered to myself. Now that I know where she works I can patiently develop my plan of action... *"So this is what it feels like to be in love,"* I thought to myself.

I couldn't get her out of my mind. So the following day I decided to ask her out on a date. The attraction was quite overpowering. I headed to the pharmacy and waited patiently outside for the right moment. I wanted to

102

make sure the store was completely empty of customers before I went in. As I entered the pharmacy, I was so nervous that I could feel the cold sweat ever so slowly, dripping down from my armpits. The girl was restocking a shelf with merchandise and had her back to me. As I began to walk towards her, I felt as though I was walking the plank on a pirate ship, each step bringing me closer to the edge. In my mind I was busy practising the words that I was going to say to her, over and over:

"Would you like to go out on a date on Saturday night?... I'd love to take you out on Saturday night, are you free?... Are you free on Saturday night?"
When she finally turned around, I bravely looked straight into her beautiful big eyes and said, *"Can I have a box of those vitamin tablets please?"*

I couldn't believe the words that came out of my mouth. What happened to the other words I was practising?... They never came out. This girl had no idea of the internal agony I was experiencing. I paid for the vitamins and left the store totally disappointed.

A couple of days later I decided to make another attempt. I was convinced that this time things would turn out much better because we were no longer strangers. After checking if the coast was clear, I entered the store, walked straight to the counter with confidence, looked directly into her big beautiful eyes, smiled and bravely said, *"Can I have a box of those vitamin tablets please?"*

I couldn't believe it. The wrong stupid words came out of my mouth again. This time however, the girl smiled and then handed me the tablets. After paying, I left the store disappointed and discouraged.

I still couldn't get her out of my mind and so a few days later, I decided to make one more last attempt. I knew this had to be it. Third time lucky. So again after checking if the coast was clear, I entered the store, walked straight to the counter with confidence, looked directly into her big beautiful eyes, smiled, she smiled back and I bravely said, *"Can I have a box of those vitamin tablets please?"*... The girl started laughing. I told her, *"They're for my Dad."* I felt so stupid, I just couldn't get the right words out. After paying for the vitamins I left the store for the third time with nothing else besides vitamins. There was no way I was going in there again and my Dad's going to kill me if he sees all these vitamin bottles!

I thought I was in love with this girl, but I realized I didn't love her enough to overcome the fear I had. My fear was greater than the love I had for her and because of it, I lost her. She ended up becoming someone else's girlfriend. If I truly loved her, the fear would never have stopped me.

At the age of nineteen I went to Canada to visit my brother. In the last week of my holiday I was invited to an anniversary party. During the party, I found myself sitting on a staircase with another guy just chatting. All of a sudden, a girl in a green outfit walked by. When she passed in front of my eyes, it was as though she put me into a trance. My heart-rate shot through the roof and I began to feel really, really strange. My heart was beating in my chest so hard that I thought everyone would hear it. I got up off the stairs and followed her. She went into the basement where everybody was gathered. I saw her sit down on the floor near the back of the room with some other girls. I asked my brother if he could see the girl in the green outfit. He said, *"Yes, why?"*... *"I'm going to marry her!"* The crazy thing was, we hadn't even met yet. I absolutely shocked my brother when I told him I needed his help to talk to her father. I wanted him to suggest an arranged marriage for the two of us if she agreed. Arranged marriages were a common thing in our Indian culture back then. He said he would talk to her father in the next few days. I was not about to wait that long, even though the only conversation I had with her that night was, *"What's your name?"* That was it.

The next day I found myself sitting in a rocking chair listening to Paul Anka love songs and praying, which was strange because at the time I was a devout atheist. I prayed a simple, but very emotional prayer. I promised God that I would believe in him if he helped me marry this girl. For the next few hours all I could do was think about her and listen to love songs. I was completely love struck.

All of a sudden, the phone rang. The caller was a friend of the girl in green. She had also been at the party that night. She was asking me for a double-date. I asked her which other girl would be joining us. She told me that it would be Rani. That was the name of the girl in green. I almost had a heart attack! I agreed. Five minutes after I put the phone down, the phone rang again. This time it was Rani herself. Now I really thought I was going to have a heart attack. She asked me if I got a call from her friend and what she had said to me. I told Rani I only agreed to go on the double-date because I had found out that she was also going. Surprisingly to me, she said, *"The only reason I was going was because I found out that you were going."* I was flabbergasted.

I suggested to her that we cancel the double-date and go on a date by ourselves. She agreed. We met the very next day and spent the whole day together. We shared so much about ourselves. It was an amazing day. That evening she went back to her house and I went back to my brother's place. When I got there, I ran straight to the phone and called her. I asked her 2 questions: *"Did you enjoy the day?"* and *"So, do you want to get married?"* She replied, *"Yes, alright!"*... I know it sounds crazy, but that's exactly what happened and by my 20th birthday we were married! Today we've been married for almost 30 years and have two wonderful sons.

By the way, I'm no longer an atheist. This is a testimony not only to the power of prayer, but to the power of love. It was the power of love that truly empowered my prayer.

Chapter 17

Power of Your Positive Past
(Formula #12)

"Every saint has a past, and every sinner has a future."
- Oscar Wilde

I've always heard people say, *"If you want to create a great future you have to forget your past. You must let go of what was negative in your past if you want to move ahead in life."* It's easy to say, but for most people it is virtually impossible to do. I have personally discovered that there is a way where, instead of trying to forget your past, you can use your past to empower yourself to build a greater future. This is how you do it... Get yourself a journal that has about 120 pages. Number each page clearly. These pages represent the potential years of your life. If you are 40 years old, you're at page 40, with all the pages on the left representing your past and all the pages on your right representing your future. There are four main things you want to record on these pages:

1. Every **SUCCESS**, minor and major, that you can remember achieving throughout your life. Maybe when you were 10-years-old you won a trophy at school for winning a race. Write it down. It's a success. The first job you were hired for, regardless of how meager the salary. Write it down. It's a success. The goal of this exercise is to dig out, from the depths of your subconscious mind, every bit of success that you've ever experienced and absolutely flood the pages of your life with it. Once you do it, you will be amazed at how empowering it will be for you to experience again, all the success that you had ever achieved and forgotten... you have brought it all back to life again.

2. Every **GREAT EXPERIENCE** that you've had in your life. Maybe you went on a vacation with your parents when you were young and you remember something wonderful that happened. Write it down. Maybe you went snorkelling in the ocean for the first time or sky diving or mountain climbing. Write it down. All these things will give you a sense of fulfilment, showing you that you have already experienced some great

things in your life. Things that you had long forgotten... and now you've brought them back to life again.

3. All the **GREAT PEOPLE** that have come into your life. A few years ago I began to trace back how exactly a particular person who had influenced my life in a great way, had come into my life. As I traced back the steps. I was shocked to discover that it all went back to this one person, let's call her Jane, whom I absolutely hated at one time in my life. Many years ago, Jane gave my name as a referral to a salesperson. That sales person led me to another person who eventually led me to the person who made a huge difference in my life. For many years I had great resentment against Jane due to personal reasons. The resentment was so strong that I couldn't even bare to be in the same room with her. Just thinking about Jane would make my blood boil.

Many years later, after going through a great amount of spiritual growth, there was a period in my life that whenever I attempted to pray, I would hear in my head, *"Why are you asking me to forgive you when you have not forgiven the person whom you have resentment against?"* It drove me crazy! Every time I prayed, I heard these words. I knew I wouldn't be able to pray again until I resolved the issue. I decided to forgive the person. However, I knew I couldn't just say, *"I forgive you"* to myself. I had to make amends face-to-face because that person probably felt the same way about me. I decided to wait until the next time we met at a family get-together and do it then.

The day finally arrived. I was invited to a family function and I knew this person would also be present. I had told the host of the house I was going to be a little late due to a business meeting. When I arrived at the house, everybody had just finished eating their appetizers. The host told me there was plenty of food remaining on the tables in the lower level of the house. As I walked down the stairs to get my food, I couldn't believe my eyes. The whole room was empty of people except for one other person who also came late, Jane. She was standing at the table getting food. Coincidence?... It seemed a little more than just coincidence. I couldn't believe how perfect the opportunity was. As I got to the table Jane turned around and said,

"Hi."... I knew this was my only chance. Before anyone else walked into the room, I had to say what I needed to say, now.

"I want to thank you... For what?... A few days ago I did an exercise where I had to trace back, how exactly a particular person who had influenced my life in a great way, had come into my life. As I traced back the steps, they led me all the way back to you. Do you remember a few years ago, you gave my name to a salesperson who was selling scholarship investments?... Yes... Well, that guy became a good friend of mine and he introduced me to another person who actually introduced me to the person who influenced my life in the greatest way. I only met that person because of you. So I wanted to thank you for making a big difference in my life."

I then gave Jane a hug. Immediately at that very moment, all the anger I was holding in my heart completely vanished. I was no longer a slave to the resentment.

At a seminar many years ago, I heard this phrase, *"As you live your life you will make many different types of friends: friends for a reason, friends for a season and friends for life."* I truly believe that God will bring key people into our life to influence and direct us along a certain path of goodness. We need to be grateful and open our eyes to see the good that each and every person brings as they cross our path, regardless of how small or large a role they play in our lives.

4. All the **STRUGGLES** you've had in your past that you have finally overcome and the lessons that you learned from them. Write them down. As you reflect back and record the painful struggles and challenges you had to go through, the purpose is not to bring back the pain but to show you how victorious you have been; to prove to yourself that despite all the pain of your challenge, you still got through it, you still overcame, you won the fight, you made it!!! Once you've recorded the challenges in your past that you have successfully overcome, not only will you gain wisdom from each experience as you reflect on them, but you will also gain tremendous power.

In the future when you experience new struggles and challenges, as you look back, you will see that you've already been through other struggles in your past that were just as tough or tougher than the one you're going through currently. Your past will now be a great source of power to you. It will push you successfully through the new challenges and struggles that enter your life. Your past is proof that you have what it takes, to make it through the tough times!

Imagine if you had a book like this from your grandparents, of all the things they went through and all the things they learnt from their tough times. How valuable would it be to you? It would be like a window through which you could see them actually living their life. It would be more powerful than a video, because you would get to read their very thoughts. How valuable would it be to your children and grandchildren to read your book. It would be one of the greatest gifts you could ever give to them. Your life in words. Your legacy.

A few years ago my younger son read a portion of my book where I had written that I had lost all my businesses and all my money. After reading it he looked at me and asked, *"This really happened to you Dad?"*... I could see by the look on his face, his respect for me increased tremendously within seconds of reading just that one page.

Every night before you go to bed, ask yourself, *"Is there anything I can write in my book? What great successes, what great experiences and what great people came into my life today?"* As you think, hope and expect to write something down each day, you will attract more great successes, more great experiences and more great people into your life.

Now, if you're thinking, I have no successes to write in my book. I haven't achieved anything special in my life whatsoever. I'm a complete loser! Even though I don't believe you, I will give you the benefit of the doubt. So let's assume you're right. There is still one success you can write in your book. Think back to the time right before you were born. You were in your mother's womb for 9 long months and when the time was right, you struggled, but successfully got out... Write that in your book!!!

Chapter 18

Manage Events, Not Time

*"If you really want the key to success, start by doing
the opposite of what everyone else is doing."*

- Brad Szollos

If you ask a 12 year old child, *"How old are you?"*, there's a good chance
their reply will be, *"Nearly 13."*
A 15 year old... *"Nearly 16."*
A 17 year old... *"Nearly 18."*
A 20 year old... *"Nearly 21."*
However, I have yet to meet a 39-year-old female who proudly says,
"Nearly 40!" You just don't hear that answer very often. Most of the young
people I meet can't wait to be older and yet almost all of the older people
want to stay at the age they're at. To the outside world birthdays are a time
of celebration, but behind closed doors the majority of older people are
quite disappointed with the way their life has turned out...

*"Another year has passed. I'm one year older. Five years ago, I had all
these dreams of where I wanted to be in life and now those five years have
come and gone, but nothing has changed. I work hard. I'm always busy. I'm
a good person, but I'm running out of time. How much **more** harder do I
have to work? How much **more** busier do I have to get? How many **more**
sacrifices do I have to keep making? I don't want to live like this, but I don't
get it, why is my life not changing?!"*

What does it take to become successful?

If you give people enough time to discover the answers for themselves,
most people will come up with the same correct answers: *"You got to have
a dream! You have to be passionate, committed, focussed, disciplined,
persistent, consistent..."* Most people already know what it takes to
become successful, but what confused me for years was why so many
people who had great success in one area did not have considerable success
in all the other areas of their life. If they are significantly successful in one

area of their life, they obviously know what it takes to become successful. Then why can't they simply apply the same success principles that caused success in that one area, to all the other areas of their life? It made no sense to me. Some of the people I met had great financial success, but their family relationships and their health was a mess. Some had great family relationships but they were broke and had poor health. Some even confessed to be very spiritual, yet had terrible family relationships and poor health.

When we ask someone who has great success in one area of their life, *"Why don't you have success in all the other areas of your life?"*, they can give us one of three possible answers:

1. *"I don't care about all the other areas of my life."*... I have yet to receive this answer from anyone, but it still remains a possibility.

2. *"To achieve great success in one area, I must sacrifice all the other areas of my life."*... I have received this answer from numerous people, however, I truly believe this is a false truth. If you are promised great financial reward for your effort, at the cost of losing your family and your health, would you still pursue it? I have not come across one person who said, *"Yes!"* No matter how much financial success you achieve, if you fail miserably in the other areas of your life, those areas will eventually steal the joy from the success you do have. You will never feel like a success even though you may look like one.

True Success is progressively winning in ALL areas of your life at the same time. Not necessarily at the same level, but at the same time. So you can proudly say to yourself that your relationship with your children is better today than it was six months ago. Your relationship with your spouse is better today than it was a year ago. Your health is better than it was 3 months ago. Your spiritual life is stronger than it was a year ago. Your finances are better than they were 2 years ago. Your performance at your job or business is better this month than it was last month. In every area of your life you can see and feel some growth. When this happens, the growth in every area collectively, even if it is small, will empower you to achieve even greater success in all areas of your life.

3. Finally, the third answer they can give us, which I believe is the truth... *"I want to, but I don't know why I don't have success in all the other areas of my life."*

What is it that people can't see? It took me many years to figure this out. What we can't see is what I call, **The Hidden Principle of Success**. Let me explain... Wherever I go around the world, I hear people talking about *'Time Management.'* It is assumed that if you become better at time management, you'll increase your chances of success. However, if you look in the dictionary under the word *'Manage,'* you will see that in order to manage something you have to be able to *'Handle it,' 'Alter it'* or *'Direct it for a particular purpose.'* So let me ask you, *"Can you handle time?, alter time?, direct time?, slow time down or speed time up?"* The answer is a categorical *"NO!"* So why does the whole world talk about *'Time Management'* when it doesn't even exist? Like parrots we keep repeating the phrase without paying attention to what we are saying.

There is no such thing as *Time Management*. There is only *Event Management*. You can only manage the events that you carry out in the time that already exists. An event is anything you do that takes time, such as taking out the trash, walking your dog or going to work.

<u>The Hidden Principle of Success</u>:
All events are either present based or future based. Present based events will keep you in the present. Future based events will cause your life to change. If you can determine which events are present based and which are future based, you can change your life.

Let me give you some examples to deepen your understanding of this philosophy.

1. A Spotless Home

Let's say you love to clean your house and you spend numerous hours a day cleaning it. You must understand, no matter how much time you spend on cleaning your house and no matter how good a job you do, it will not cause you to move into a mansion. Cleaning your home is a present based event.

2. Business Success

In the Network Marketing industry, if you ask any of the top level achievers what you should do to become successful, they will all say the same things. Besides buying and selling products, you need to do five things: listen to CDs, read books, associate with the leaders, contact new prospects and show the business plan.

Out of the five, only one will be the future based event and all the remaining four will be present based. There is always only ONE true future based event in each set of events that need to be done to achieve a particular goal.

How do we identify which event is the future based event?

You identify it by isolating each event and asking yourself, *"If I only do this event is there any chance of achieving my goal?"*

Well, let's see... If you listen to 5 CDs each and every day, but you never do what you're told to do by the speakers on the CDs, will you become successful? Obviously not... so, *listening to CDs* is a present based event. If you read the recommended books each and every day, but you never do what you're told to do by the authors of the books, will you become successful? Obviously not... so, *reading books* is a present based event. If you attend all the seminars & conventions put on by your leaders, but never do what you're told to do by the speakers on the stage, will you become successful? Obviously not... so, *associating with the leaders* is still yet another present based event.

If you *show the plan...* and then *show the plan...* and then *show the plan...* will you achieve your goal? Most people would say, *"Yes!"* There are numerous people who believe that showing the plan is the most important thing they can possibly do to build their business, but the first thing they do is the exact opposite. They decide NOT to show it until they can do it absolutely perfectly; until they become the very best at showing the plan. They set up a white board and easel, half a dozen chairs and then carefully seat the prospects, their favourite cuddly teddy bears, in the chairs and begin, *"Do you have a dream? I can help you achieve it. Together we can do it! You can be financially free!"*

Unfortunately, no matter how good you get at showing your business plan, those teddy bears are not going to resurrect and join you in your business. The ultimate consequence of showing the plan over and over again, is that you will have no more plans to show, until you contact new prospects to show the plan to. The act of showing the plan is not the future based event. *CONTACTING* new prospects is the future based event. I will prove it to you.

Let's assume that you don't know how to show the plan and instead of trying to learn and become a great presenter, you learn, practice and become a great *contacter.* You then consistently contact anyone who gets within 10 feet of you... you become an 'animal' at contacting. By the end of the month you have 100 people interested in looking at your business presentation. If you called one of your up-line team members and told them that you have 100 people waiting to see the plan and you need help, what do you think they'll say? Obviously they'll be very excited and willing to make a presentation for you. After the presentation, if only 6 to 10 people decide to get registered and seriously build their businesses, will you be successful? Of course you will. This proves that contacting is the true future based event.

3. Becoming an A+ Student

After miserably failing his year-end exams at school, a 14 year old boy promises his parents that he will study for three hours every day after school to get his grades back up. His parents, after hearing his commitment, become hopeful and proud, *"What a good boy. Next year his grades will be so much better now that he is determined to study hard."* On the first day of his new goal, after arriving home, the boy runs up the stairs and heads straight into his room determined to put his 3 hours of studying in. He grabs his school bag, places it on his bed and begins to slowly empty the contents. Every time he takes something out of his bag it seems to grab his attention for a moment or two. I'm sure there's a story behind every item...

A bottle of water... *"It's full. I thought I drank most of this."*
Half a sandwich... *"Oh, I forgot to eat the rest of that. I wonder why?"*
Another bottle of water... *"Here it is. I didn't know I had 2 bottles of water."*
A black banana... *"Gross! How long has this been in my bag?"*
Another bottle of water... *"No wonder my bag felt heavy."*
A crumpled up piece of paper... *"I wonder what this is?"*

Twenty minutes later, he finally empties the contents of his bag onto his bed. What a mess. He gathers the books he needs and takes them over to his desk. As he puts them down, he notices out of the corner of his right eye that his closet door is open. It triggers a thought, *"I wonder what I should wear tomorrow?"* That's all it took, one thought. All of a sudden, he's got clothes all over the bed, the desk and the chair. It's as though he's having a fashion show.

Twenty minutes later, he's finally picked out his outfit for tomorrow and coincidently right at that very moment he hears a 'ping.' It's a Facebook notification. He just received a message from a friend of his. Of course it's probably urgent and must be looked at immediately. As he does, he gets distracted by all the pictures... Twenty minutes later he forces himself to stop looking at the never ending pictures. He then reaches over and grabs his folder containing notes on his latest project. As he flips the pages he realizes that his writing is very messy and decides to rewrite some of his notes.

Finally, a little while later, he picks up one of his textbooks and starts to study the actual content that he was supposed to be studying. Twenty minutes later he looks at his watch and says to himself with great pride,

"Right on track!... 3 hours." This boy has absolutely no idea what's happening. He will continue to fail again and again until he realizes what exactly he's doing wrong. If he knew about present based and future based events he would approach his studying completely differently.

He would walk into his room saying to himself, *"Future based events only!"* He would open up his bag and take out only what he needs in order to study. He would close the closet door as he repeats to himself, *"This is a trap! This is present based."* He would switch off Facebook as he says to himself again, *"This is a trap! It's present based."* He would then open his textbook as he says to himself, *"This is future based! This is the only thing that will change my grades!"*

Within 5 minutes he is studying and on track to getting better grades because he now knows what will keep him in the present and more importantly what will cause his life to change. I know this situation very well because this 14-year-old boy is me. I wrestled with focus all the time when I was a teenager. I failed most of my exams and never made it to university because I couldn't focus on studying. If I had learned this philosophy earlier on in my life, it would have helped me tremendously in so many ways.

4. Health

There are many people who want to be fitter & healthier. In order to achieve this goal it's a common understanding that we must do a combination of three things: change our diet, reduce the size of our meals and exercise. Most people however, decide to change only their diet and believe they can be successful by doing just this one thing. Unfortunately, most of the people who fail to stick to a diet, fail because they simply love food too much. The very thing they absolutely love is the thing they are trying to give up 'cold turkey' and for most people, this will never work.

Exercising is the future based event and if we focus all our energy on developing a consistent exercise program, we can eat whatever we want. We don't have to fight with the foods we love. I will prove it to you... I have the best exercise program you'll ever see, you will love it if you love food.

It will allow you to eat whatever you want to eat, even the most greasy, disgustingly delicious foods you can dream of. The first thing you do is prepare the dish you love to eat the most. The food that you know you should not be eating. The most unhealthy delightfully tasting feast. Maybe it's a slab of bacon with a crisp half inch thick border of juicy fat, or cheddar covered potato skins drowning in sour cream, or crispy breaded wings with the skin still on them and covered in hot buffalo sauce with a cup of thick ranch dressing to dip them into, or a Big Mac with fries and a large coke, or a deep pan meatball pizza with triple cheese, cheese in the crust, cheese-flavoured dipping sauce on the side and a thick strawberry milkshake. Whatever it is, get ready to enjoy it right after your exercise program. Doesn't this sound too good to be true?... like you've died and gone to your favourite restaurant in heaven?

Once you've got your meal ready, place it on a table with a fan blowing gently above it, so you can smell the beautiful aroma on the other side of the room where you will be exercising. Then get into your shorts & T-shirt and begin your first 15-minute exercise program... Push-ups! Sit-ups! Jogging on the spot! For a total of 15 minutes. At the end of your 15 minutes, as you are slightly panting, carefully make your way to your feast and enjoy! Wasn't that painless and very rewarding? Continue this 15 minute workout routine every other day for a week.

The following week, get your meal ready again, place it on the table, turn on the fan, get into your shorts & T-shirt and begin your exercise program. This time however, you need to do it for 20 minutes. Push-ups! Sit-ups! Jogging on the spot!... After 20 minutes you'll be panting a fair amount and one bead of sweat will eventually escape from a pore in your forehead and slowly drip down your face. As you pant and catch your breath, you carefully make your way over to your feast and enjoy. This time however, even though you are enjoying your meal, for some strange reason you're beginning to feel a sense of guilt for eating it, but you don't know why and where it's coming from. After a couple of bites you begin to lose your appetite and can only finish half of your meal. Something mysterious is beginning to happen inside of your body. Continue this 20 minute workout routine every other day for a week.

Now it's the beginning of the third week. Get your meal ready again, place it on the table, turn on the fan, get into your shorts & T-shirt and begin your exercise program. This time however, you need to do it for 30 minutes. Push-ups! Sit-ups! Jogging on the spot!... After 30 minutes you'll be panting like a dog on a hot summer day! Sweat will be pouring down your face like a mini-waterfall! Your heart will be pumping so fast and so loud that you'll hear the vibration in your ears like a band of drums! As you try to breathe deeper and faster to catch your breath, the only oxygen you get is the aroma from your fat-filled meal going down your lungs and trying to suffocate you! As you get closer and closer to your meal, it gets harder and harder for you to breathe. Once you're there, leaning over your meal, you hear a scream in your ears, just like the scream you heard in a horror movie when you were a child.

"Don't you dare put that in your mouth! Don't you dare put that into me! Don't you know how hard I worked? Don't do it!"... Your body pleads with you to not put that disgusting food into your mouth. It doesn't need it. It doesn't want it. All of a sudden an uncontrollable violent urge makes you pick up the plate and throw it across the room as far as you can... *"I ain't eating this crap no more!"*, you shout to yourself.

Congratulations, you're on your way to a fitter and healthier body. When you focus your efforts on a consistent exercise program, which is the future based event, you no longer have to fight the urges of your favourite foods with your mind alone, your body will take the lead.

5. Family

I am sure that all new moms and dads say to themselves, *"I want to have a great family."* I said the same thing. As my boys were growing up, I wanted to make sure I had a great relationship with each of them. Every Sunday, my wife and I would take them out somewhere and spend time having fun, trying to build those family bonds. Years later, as my boys got older, after many 'family days,' I felt as though I was losing my kids. The closeness wasn't there anymore. That's when I came to the realization that 'family day' was not the future based event that kept the family together.

If a teenager has a personal problem, he or she is not going to bring it up on family day in front of all the others kids. They're going to keep it inside or share it with someone else besides their parents, someone who makes time for them personally. The highest suicide rates are from the ages of 15 to 24. This is the age when these youngsters begin to realize that the challenges of life can get quite overwhelming, especially if you don't have the right support system. Unfortunately, not only do many parents not set aside personal time for their children, but so many don't know how to build these relationships because their parents never set the example.

So what is the future based event for building a great family?

In the Network Marketing industry when an Independent Business Owner wants to show their marketing plan to a new prospect, the first thing they do is set up an appointment. Most of the time it is one-on-one with an individual or a couple. Upon getting together, every effort is made to eliminate any potential distractions during the meeting: pets, small children, phones and TV. Once the environment is set, the Business Owner begins the presentation. All throughout the presentation the Business Owner pays great attention to actively listening to the needs and concerns of the prospect as he pours out his heart in an effort to connect.

This is exactly how you build great relationships and in turn a great family. You set up one-on-one appointments with each member of your family. With each son, each daughter, each grandparent and your spouse. Each and every person that makes up your family that you say you care and love, you make an appointment with them. The goal of the appointment should be focussed on the depth of the conversation. Superficial conversations have no power to make a heart-to-heart connection.

"How was school today?"... "Good."
"How is your homework going?"... "Good."
"How's your life?"... "Good."
"Good!"

This was a typical conversation I had with my kids when they were younger. There's absolutely no depth or power of connection in this dialogue. When I finally realized that I needed to make an appointment to build the relationships in my family, I said to my oldest son, who was 16 at the time, *"I want to make an appointment with you on Sunday at 3:00pm."*... *"What?"*... *"We need to talk, note it down. Sunday at 3:00pm in your room."*... *"Okay."*... My son had a very strange look on his face, full of hesitant curiosity.

Sunday came. I went into his room and we began the appointment. I told my son even though I'm his dad and much older than he is, it wasn't too far back that I was 16 just like he is today. And when I was his age, I also had the same thoughts that he currently has in his head. I told him I knew exactly what he was thinking because I've been in his shoes. Then I began to tell him a little about my younger days. I could see he was very interested by the way he was eagerly listening to every word. It was like telling him secrets of my past. Everybody likes to hear secrets. I kept talking and he kept listening. Then I told him about all the stupid things I did and thought about doing when I was his age, and that's when his jaw dropped. Hopefully he was thinking, *"My dad's just like me, he does understand!"* Thirty minutes were up... *"We've ran out of time, it's 3:30pm. We can continue next Sunday, same time."*

The following Sunday arrived. I went into his room and continued from where we left off. After about five minutes or so, my son starting talking... and talking... and talking. He wouldn't shut up. He started telling me about every stupid thing he was thinking of doing and this time, it was my jaw that dropped.

The more appointments we had, the closer our relationship got. I could tell that we were connecting. The conversations were getting deeper and deeper. A few weeks later I was looking out the window, expecting to see my son arriving from school. When I eventually saw him, I noticed that he was walking towards our front door with a friend of his. I expected him to come in right away, but he didn't. He stood outside having a conversation for quite a while. When he eventually came in, I asked what he was doing outside. He told me that his friend didn't have a dad and he was telling him about our appointments. Then after he did this, his friend had some questions and my son was helping to answer them. When I heard this, I knew for sure setting up appointments was definitely the future based event for building a great family... this was proof!

6. Spiritual Growth

Many people say they want to grow spiritually, but don't know how. There are three things that will help us grow spiritually: reading scripture, attending a place of worship and prayer. However, only one is the future based event.

If we attend a place of worship and read scripture, we will grow intellectually. Our mind will increase in knowledge. However, the only way to truly grow spiritually is to grow your heart and that is done through constant prayer. Prayer is the intelligence of the heart. Reading scripture and attending a place of worship will teach you how to pray more effectively, but only prayer will connect you with your Heavenly Father's heart. This connection is what causes your heart to grow.

Chapter 19

Practical Application of Event Management

"One of the very worst uses of time is to do something very well, that need not be done at all."

- Brian Tracy

Now that we have a deeper understanding of future based and present based events, what do we do next? How do we actually apply this philosophy into our life practically?

The first step is to make a list of each and every thing we do on a daily, weekly and monthly basis. Whatever it is, we need to list it; everything that takes time to do. Secondly we need to identify and circle all the future based events. Third, in our planner, we need to block off the times of all the fixed events that we cannot change. For example, if we go to work from 9 to 5, we need to block off that time slot because we can't adjust it. Once we do this, we'll be able to see all the flexible time slots remaining that we can input our events into. Fourth, now we need to input all our future based events into our planner and FIX them. This means to allocate and commit a specific time for each future based event which cannot be changed. Some of these events will be daily, some weekly and some monthly, according to your goals. The key thing to remember as we fill our planner is to...

ALWAYS INPUT FIRST, THAT WHICH CREATES YOUR FUTURE... AND THEN FIX IT!

Lastly, input all the present based events into the time slots remaining. If we follow the above order of inputting events, we will be guaranteeing that our life will change, because we are doing exactly that which creates change in our life. A lot of people will say, *"I already make a list everyday of the things I need to do, so what's the difference between making a list and doing the above?"* When you make a list, all the events are 'floating.' There is no commitment to a particular time slot and more importantly, to the order in which we do the events... we are prone to procrastination. At the end of the day, most people will have certain events remaining that they

122

didn't get to do and so they will move them to the next day. At the end of the following day, there are again a few events that were not done and so again they will be carried over to the next day... and so on and so forth.

If you carefully review the events that you keep carrying to the following day, you will most likely discover they are future based events. The events that will cause your life to change are the very events that you are not doing, and 5 years later, most people will wonder in amazement, *"Why is my life not changing?"* I did this for years. I always made a list and found myself procrastinating without being aware that I was doing it. But why do we procrastinate?

When water travels, what path does it take? Water always takes the path of least resistance. You'll never find water trying to do something difficult like going up a wall. How much water is in a human body? Let's say 70%. Well then, if we are 70% water, when we make a list of things to do, 70% of the time we will behave like water, we will also take the path of least resistance.

A few years ago, I remember this one particular day vividly. I was in my office. I had pictures of my dreams plastered all over the walls. I had a binder on my desk, bursting with yet more pictures of beautiful dreams. All these dreams and yet I still couldn't get myself to do the key things I needed to do to achieve my goals. I couldn't stop procrastinating, especially when it came to picking up the phone and making calls to prospective business leads. I just couldn't pick up the phone consistently. It was as though there was something inside of me that was trying to stop me from doing the very things that would cause me to achieve my goals and change my life. This thing inside of me felt like a manipulative and debilitating disease. If I could only see it, I could then figure out a way to somehow destroy it or at least get it out of me. In an attempt to understand it better, I developed a definition of what I believed procrastination to be...

Procrastination is an invisible disease that takes hold of a talented individual with great potential and turns that person slowly, bit by bit, over time, into a complete and utter failure.

On this one particular day, as I was struggling greatly to pick up the phone, I imagined the disease as a little green man with big teeth, standing behind me against the back wall of my office. He started talking to me.

"Hey Terry, you've worked so hard all day. You know there's a beautiful warm bed in the other room. Why don't you take a ten minute nap and then you'll have all the energy you need to make your calls?... Hey Terry, do you hear your kids downstairs? They're missing you. Come on, be a good father and go down and spend some time with them... Hey Terry, do you hear that noise? It's the TV. Your favourite TV program, 'Everybody Loves Raymond' is on. Go down and watch it before it finishes. You know how much it makes you laugh... Hey Terry, do you hear that noise? It's your stomach rumbling. Hurry up, go downstairs and eat something before you starve to death!"

This little green man kept yapping away... *"Yap! Yap! Yap!"* He was driving me crazy!... *"Shut up and leave me alone!"* I would scream. After being bombarded by constant manipulative verbiage, I would eventually get up and head to the door. As I closed the door on my way out, to go and do exactly what he was enticing me to do, I could hear him giggling away in an evil manner, *"Ha! Ha! Ha! I got you again!"*

I had to make this disease, this little green man, as real as possible. It was the only way I could hope to defeat the disease of procrastination. This little green man, like a vile disease, had a specific intent. His goal was to destroy my future, but he knew he couldn't come running at me head on, otherwise I would stop him in his tracks. Instead, he would attack discretely. Not only was I unaware of what he was trying to do, but I would not even know of his existence until years later.

Small steps. Small distractions. Everyday a little nudge. Everyday a little distraction to get me slightly off course. *"Go and play with your kids!... Go and eat something!... You're tired, take a rest!"* Every week! Every month! Month after month of distractions. Year after year of distractions. 3 Years, 5 years, 10 years and eventually he would stand victorious and declare to himself, *"I have done it! Mission accomplished. I have completely destroyed his future!"*

Chapter 20

Power to Overcome Procrastination

"Procrastination is like a credit card: it's a lot of fun until you get the bill."

- Christopher Parker

Where do you get the power and confidence to overcome procrastination, the little green man? There are 3 main sources of power:

1. MIND-SET
Program your mind to help you fight procrastination. Repeat to yourself, over and over again...

"I ALWAYS DO FIRST THAT WHICH CREATES MY FUTURE!"

As you flood your mind with this statement, you will be constantly reminded to stay on track. There will come many a time when you will be tempted to do something that you know you should not be doing, and at that very moment, as you're about to do it, you will hear in your head, *"I always do first that which creates my future!"* If that voice is strong enough, from constant repetition, it will cause you to stop and do instead, that which you should be doing.

2. CONSEQUENCE
After returning home from a very powerful motivational seminar, Peter sat quietly on the edge of his bed. He was thinking about what he had just experienced. He was truly moved... *"That's it, it's time to take my business to the next level. No more games. I'm going to get on the phone tomorrow night at 8.00pm and make some prospecting calls. I'm going Diamond!"* Peter truly believed that his life was about to change.

Even though there was no one else physically in the room with Peter when he made the decision to start building his business seriously, there was someone listening. The little green man has a big brother, the GIANT. The only purpose of his existence is to record each & every promise a person

125

makes and whether or not it is kept or broken. The GIANT stores the results of our promises in our subconscious mind.

When Peter said to himself, *"Tomorrow night, I'm going to make prospecting calls,"* the GIANT made a note of it. *"Got it! Tomorrow night you have promised to make prospecting calls at 8:00pm."*

The next morning upon awakening, as Peter moves the covers aside and stands up, the GIANT comes running. He jumps onto Peter's back, puts his arms around his neck and wraps his legs around his waist. He then reminds Peter of the promise he made last night... *"Don't forget, you said you're going to make phone calls tonight at 8:00pm, because you're going Diamond!"*

By the afternoon, Peter starts feeling pretty tired. He thinks it's because of all the work he's done, but that's not the reason why. He's been carrying the GIANT on his back all day long. The GIANT has been constantly reminding him of the promise he made.

When Peter got home that night he was feeling very anxious. It seemed like the clock was ticking faster than normal. All of a sudden it was already 7:45pm. Peter was getting very nervous. *"There must be something more important that needs to be done right now,"* he thought to himself... *"There must be something!"*... it was 7:59pm... *"Yes, I have to help the kids with their homework!"* He was very relieved as he came up with this great discovery all by himself.

As Peter attempted to help his kids with their homework, they asked him, *"Dad, what are you doing?"*... *"I'm helping you with your homework."*... *"We don't need your help."*... *"Yes you do! Yes you do!"* As Peter sat there with his kids, he began to feel a tremendous sickening feeling in his gut. He knew he shouldn't be there, he should be making the calls. He kept glancing at his watch. It was now 8:45pm. The guilt was still swirling inside of him. Fifteen more minutes of this agony, he thought to himself. His heart was racing as a cold sweat took a hold of his body. Finally his watch displayed 9:00pm and Peter lets out a big sigh of relief. *"Ahhhh, even if I wanted to make calls, it's too late now. I'll definitely make the calls tomorrow at 8:00pm, because I'm going Diamond!"*

Peter convinces himself that it's okay to start again after failing to achieve a goal. *"All you have to do is reset it and go again,"* he tells himself. Later that night Peter decides to go to bed. As he puts his left leg under the covers, another leg goes into the bed, but it's not his. Then as he puts his right leg under the covers, another leg goes into the bed again. It's the GIANT's legs. He's still on Peter's back. The GIANT will be sleeping with Peter all night. He represents the guilt Peter feels for not keeping his word.

As Peter tosses and turns, the GIANT tosses and turns with him. He's still got Peter by the neck and the waist. All night he reminds Peter of his broken promises: *"You said you were going to make the calls and you didn't! You said you were going to build your business and take your children to Disney World. You told your wife you were going to free her from her job. You told your up-line leader you were going to show the plan five times a week."* All throughout the night the GIANT stabs Peter with the pangs of his own broken promises.

A few months later Peter attended another very powerful business seminar. After the event on Saturday night he went up to his hotel room. As he entered the room he felt so empowered. He whispered to himself very quietly, *"This is it, I'm going Diamond!"* All of a sudden, deep inside Peter's core, he felt a roar building up in his body. It was as if there was an earthquake happening inside of him. A thundering explosion went off in his ears. His GIANT screamed...

"You are not going Diamond! You are a liar! You are a fake! You have no integrity! Every promise you make, everything you say you're going to do, you never do it! You never keep your word! You are not going Diamond!"

The GIANT simply screamed back the truth. Every broken word, every broken promise that Peter was the cause of, was stored in his subconscious mind. As Peter heard back the discouraging footsteps of his track record, it sucked out all the energy from his decision to build his business and within moments the power he had received from the seminar was completely

127

replaced with doubt. If Peter had been aware that all his promises, broken or kept, would be stored in his subconscious mind and would be used against him or for him in the future, I am sure he would be very careful about keeping his word. If every time after Peter said he was going to do something, he did it, the results would have been completely different in that hotel room after the seminar.

Over the next few months, Peter began to realize where he was going wrong. He made a commitment to himself to never break his word again. He was determined to keep his promises. If he said he was going to do something, he made sure he did it.

A year later Peter attended another very powerful business seminar. After the event on Saturday night he went up to his hotel room. As he entered the room he felt very empowered. He whispered to himself quietly, *"This is it, I'm going Diamond!"* All of a sudden, deep within Peter, he felt a roar building up in his body. It was as if there was an earthquake happening inside of him. Then a thundering explosion went off in his ears. His GIANT was cheering him on...

"Yes, you are going Diamond because you always keep your word! Whatever you say you're going to do, you always do it, every time! Every promise you make, you always keep it. You always keep your word! You're going Diamond!"

Again, the GIANT simply screamed back the truth, but this time he supported Peter's goal. It was completely empowering. Within moments Peter went from being super excited to *"It's done!"* He knew, deep down, this was it. He was about to become a Diamond.

3. SPIRITUAL MOTIVATION

The most powerful form of motivation does not come from a book, CD or a video. It comes from consistent association with the power source. The power source are the people who have achieved what you are aspiring to achieve. The people who live the way you want to live, that have done what you want to do. When you put yourself in this unique environment of power, you are prone to be affected in the most powerful of ways.

When you associate with the leaders in your field at seminars and conventions that are designed to empower future leaders, all your senses will be bombarded and stimulated at the same time. You will see the success, you will hear the wisdom, you will taste the excitement and you will feel the power & passion. As all your senses are being stimulated simultaneously your 'soul will be stirred.' Something magical will happen inside of you that you will not be able to describe. Almost like a switch being turned on inside of you. You will no longer be the same person. When that switch gets turned on inside of you, two major things are going to happen to you:

1. Absolute Belief

Sooner or later, at one of these conventions, something powerful will happen to you internally. You won't be able to explain it to anyone, but you will walk out with an unprecedented sense of belief. You will feel deep down inside your core, that you know this is the best thing that you could be doing with your life. Wherever you go, whomever you meet, the belief inside your core will radiate from inside your body and out through your eyes, and you'll start attracting people to you like a magnet.

People only follow those who have great belief. People are always looking for leaders, someone who will lead them to a better life. If you truly believe in what you are doing and what you stand for, people will follow you.

2. Absolute Power and Confidence

When your internal switch gets turned on, you will be empowered with absolute power and confidence to overcome any obstacle that gets in your way. Everything will begin to look convenient... *"Drive 5 hours? No big deal, I'll listen to 5 CDs and I'll be there!"*

You'll start looking at your goals with laser like focus, like an animal in the hunt. Nobody will be able to stop you from achieving your goals, especially the little green man... He'll be gone forever!!!

Chapter 21

Hidden Treasure

"For disappearing acts, it's hard to beat what happens to the eight hours supposedly left after eight of sleep and eight of work."

- Doug Larsen

Many people think that the purpose of their planner is to keep track of their appointments. This is obviously the reason why most people have a planner, but it is not the most important reason for having one. The true purpose of a planner has nothing to do with keeping track of your appointments. Your planner is a self-discovery tool. Its purpose is to show you who you are, how you're behaving and where you are headed.

In the movie 'Jerry McGuire' there is a famous line, *"Show me the money!"* Whenever I hear people say, *"I'm going to achieve my goal"* or *"I'm going Diamond,"* I always say, ***"Show me your planner!"***

Your planner will tell me when you listen to CDs.
Your planner will tell me when you read books.
Your planner will tell me when you pray.
Your planner will tell me when you exercise.
Your planner will tell me when you spend time with your family.
Your planner will tell me when you make phone calls.
Your planner will tell me when you show the plan.
Your planner will tell me when you follow up.
You don't have to say anything...
Your planner will reveal your true intentions.
Your planner will tell me where you're headed.
Your planner will tell me if you're going to achieve your goals.
Your planner will tell me if you're going *Diamond* or not.

If in the nearest park to your home, there lays buried 10 million dollars of gold bars in a chest. This hidden treasure has no value to you until you find it. When you glance at the pages of a person's planner, you will see all the things they have written in it. However, the most important part of each page of the planner is not what they have written, but the empty spaces that surround the events. The empty spaces are the hidden treasure. However, they have no value to you until you find them. This treasure is none other than *time* itself. The more empty spaces you're able to see, the more time you will be empowered with.

During a coaching session a few years ago, I asked my client, David, if he had any hobbies that he was passionate about... *"Painting! I absolutely love to paint. When I paint it makes me feel so connected with nature. It's as though I get transported to another world where I get to be God and create my own universe out of paint."* Wow, I didn't expect that answer.

"So, when did you last paint?... 15 years ago... What? 15 years, how comes it's been so long?... I've been too busy with work and now I have no time because I'm going Diamond!... You love painting so much, so why don't you paint for just one hour a week?... I can't! I'm going Diamond! When I'm Diamond, then I'll paint!" David replies with a deep determined aggressive tone.

David was doing what I've seen so many people, including myself do. He has a goal that he desperately wants to achieve and feels he has to give up everything that could possibly take time away from achieving it, regardless of what impact it could have on him emotionally. It's as though he opened the closet and put his painting accessories in it... then his golf clubs in it... then his fishing equipment in it... then his tennis rackets in it... then his wife in it... then his kids in it. He put everything he loved in the closet and closed the door shut. Then through the key hole he whispered, *"I'll be back when I'm Diamond!"*

David was absolutely determined to sacrifice anything and everything that could possibly get in the way of achieving his goal, but he failed to see one very important factor, his demeanor. Even though he was determined to achieve his goal, he looked totally miserable. It looked as though he had no joy in his heart. Who in their right mind would be attracted by David's demeanor? His whole business was about relating and attracting people and he was unconsciously repelling them. The thing that would give him joy, he put away, thinking it was a hindrance. What he failed to realize was that the very thing that gave him joy, was actually a tool that would compliment his ability to attract people. David put painting aside not because he wanted to sacrifice the joy it would give him, but because he thought he had no time for it. When he looked at his planner he only saw the events that were written in it, he couldn't see the treasure. He couldn't see the empty spaces of time that were buried, yet still available.

As David began to realize that there was a lot more time available to him than he thought previously, his demeanor changed. All of a sudden he was looking forward to spending time painting. His journey to *Diamond* became fun again. He would walk around thinking to himself, *"10 more days and I get to paint, can't wait... 5 more days and I get to paint... Tomorrow, I get to paint, yes!"* It wasn't long before the joy came back into David's heart and people would ask him, *"What are you so happy about?"... "Painting! I love to paint."... "Hey, so do I."...* The joy David began to experience as he pursued his passion once more began to attract joyful people into his life; people that he could then share his business opportunity with.

Over the years, I have met many people in the Network Marketing industry who have done the same thing as David, but in regards to their family. Once they discover that they can build a business and achieve financial freedom, they somewhat begin to neglect their spouse and children in pursuit of this great dream, and the very people they are building their business for become negative from that neglect. Once a person discovers how to dig up the treasure in their planner, they will realize there is time for every important thing in their life. If you set aside time for your spouse and time for your children, not only will you realize that there is plenty of time left to build your business and achieve your goals, but now your family will greatly support and encourage you in pursuit of those dreams. Once their needs are met, your children will be pushing you out the door, shouting *"Go Diamond Daddy!"...* Instead of managing your time, if you start managing and prioritizing your events, you will come up with the same two conclusions that I did:

1. There is always time for every important thing in your life.
2. You can achieve success in all areas of your life at the <u>same</u> time.

Chapter 22

Power of the Mind

"If you correct your mind, the rest of your life will fall into place."

- Lao Tzu

I once heard a pilot say that when a plane is in the air, 95% of the time it is actually off course. The pilots have to constantly repeat the same procedures over and over again to keep it on course.

The purpose of educational & motivational information, whether it be in the form of CDs, videos, books or live seminars, is not only to learn new things, but it is *the repetition of the content* that is needed to keep us on course.

A regretful man went to church to make a confession to his priest. He told the priest that he had verbally abused his wife after losing his temper and that he was very sorry and hoping God would forgive him. *"I will never do it again, I promise!"* Only an hour had passed and no sooner was he doing it again.

Most of the time, it is not a lack of knowledge that causes eventual failure, but the ability to stay on course.

"I know what to do, I just can't get myself to do it!
How can I get myself to do what I need to do?"

... Sound familiar?

The struggle we face is the struggle between our mind and body. Our mind knows what to do, but for some reason we can't get our body to co-operate and do it. There seems to be a conflict between the desires of our mind and the desires of our body. How can we unify them and get them to work together?

In reference to the diagram below...
Our body is protected and guided by our feelings.
Our mind is protected and guided by our conscience.
Our body has selfish goals ONLY: to eat, sleep, reproduce and relax.
Our mind has goals: to serve, not only our own needs but to serve the needs of others. However, it can only carry out these actions if it can get the body to do what needs to be done.

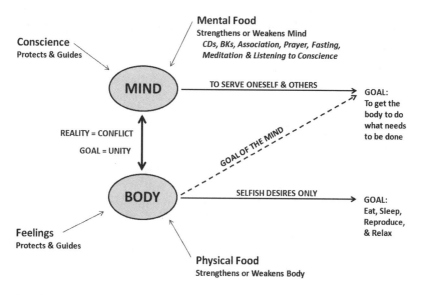

So what determines who gets their way?... Whoever is stronger will control the other.

The physical food given to the body will either strengthen or weaken it. The mental food given to the mind will either strengthen or weaken it.

The key is to strengthen your mind. The stronger the mind, the more control you will have over your body. But how do we strengthen our mind?

Positive CDs, books and association, prayer, fasting, meditation and listening to your conscience... These are the mental foods that will contribute to developing a stronger mind.

In the movie 'Cinderella Man,' there is a scene where James Braddock, the boxer, is fighting in the ring with an opponent who is much bigger than him. His coach knew that James stood no chance of beating him physically because he was too big and much stronger. He told James, "*You have to beat him from the inside out!*"... It became a battle of the minds.

The coach knew that the only way he could help James was to somehow distract the other boxer and get him to lose his concentration. By doing this, he would weaken the control that his mind had over his body and then James could finish the job.

A man with a strong mind and a weak body will always defeat a man with a strong body and weak mind.

The end goal however, is not to actually defeat your own body but to unify with it. Mind & body UNITY is the ultimate goal...

MIND: "*Body, we need to exercise. I know you're tired and you want to be fed, but this is important. We both need to work together. I need you to be healthy and fit so I can carry out my mission. I will feed you after we've done our work-out. You'll be fine, just trust me, let's do it together.*"

BODY: "*Okay, I trust you.*"

135

Chapter 23

Prepare to be a Leader

"If your actions create a legacy that inspires others to dream more, learn more, do more and become more, then you are an excellent leader."

- Dolly Parton

In order to accomplish something great in this world you need people, you can't do it by yourself. The ability to influence people to join you in your *cause*, whatever that may be, is called leadership. The greater a leader you become, the greater the level of success you will achieve in business, at your job, in your community and in your home.

There are many institutions that teach leadership. However, one of the most difficult places to be a leader and probably the best place to learn, understand and practice true leadership is in your own home, as a parent. The very day you become a parent, you automatically inherit the leadership role and title of *father* or *mother* to your newborn. As a parent you start off in the role of a positional leader to your child and can lead them by your title alone. Most little boys at the age of 3 or 4 believe their father is a superhero. Whatever he says, they believe. However, as they grow up and become more observant, they begin to realize, *"My dad ain't no Superman."* As they get older they start to notice all the weaknesses of their parents. How can they not? It's all in front of their eyes.

The home environment is a very difficult place to lead because this is the very place a parent wants to relax, kick their feet up, dress however they want to dress and many times, because no one of *importance* is watching, they will drop their guard. They will have a tendency to be a little less patient with other family members and even lose their temper more easily than they would with a co-worker. Some may even become careless with their words because they think they can. However, there *is* someone watching, who is even more important than a co-worker. Everything is on show for your children to witness and judge.

When a person is in a leadership role outside of their home, the people they are trying to lead are not being swayed negatively by the personal weaknesses of their leader, as they would have if they had been living in their home with them. Thus, leading is easier.

As the weaknesses of the parents are more and more exposed, it becomes harder for them to lead by their title alone. When the children approach their teenage years, in order for the parents to be able to continue leading them with influence, they must now earn their leadership. From personal experience, I have found there are three things that a parent must do if they want to continue to lead their children with influence:

1. Your Example
Anytime you tell your children to do something, you better be doing it yourself, otherwise, not only will you lose credibility in the area of concern, but it may cause you to also lose your ability to influence them in other areas.

2. Your Communication Skills
You must learn to talk to your children in the way their personality best receives communication. In order to get your child to better respond to you, it may be as simple as changing the way you talk to them. Learning about different personality types such as those mentioned in Dr. Robert Rohm's book, 'Personality Profiles - D.I.S.C.', is a great way to improve your communication skills.

3. Your Compassion
You may say you love your child, but if your child doesn't feel loved, they won't care what you say. Love is the greatest influencer. You must learn how to show love to your child in the unique way that will make them feel loved. The 'Five Love Languages' by Gary Chapman, portrays this beautifully. Do you know your child's love language?... *Words of affirmation, quality time, receiving gifts, physical touch or acts of service.* The only true proof that you love your child is to ask your child if they feel loved. If they don't feel loved, it doesn't really matter what you think, does it?

Why is it important to be a leader?

Sooner or later each one of us is going to follow and be influenced by someone. Your kids are going to follow someone. Your new team members are going to follow someone. You can either take responsibility to be the best leader for those people, or you can relinquish the responsibility and allow someone else to provide the leadership, at the risk that they may not be a good leader.

We often hear that we need to prepare for the tough times, but as a leader it's just as important to also prepare for the good times. When things are going great, enjoy your success, but be very careful not to get lazy and careless. Many achievers, once they've achieved a high level of success make a grave mistake; they stop doing the very things that caused their success. Many years ago, I had a number of retail stores. When I achieved a comfortable level of success, I got lazy and stopped checking the inventory. Years later after those businesses collapsed, I met up with a former employee of mine. She told me that when she worked for me, she witnessed another employee stealing hundreds of dollars out of the cash register every weekend. She couldn't tell me, because he threatened to kill her after he found out that she knew. Even though he stole from me, I was the one who created the environment for him to steal. I got lazy and stopped checking the inventory and he knew that if he took money, I wouldn't be able to tell.

In the Network Marketing industry, I've seen big leaders who had huge organizations of people and made lots of money. Then all of a sudden once they got to the top, they stopped reading books and stopped listening to CDs. They arrogantly assumed the attitude that they *knew it all* and began to slowly get off course without even knowing it. Without the influence of books and CDs, they lost the filter behind the words that came out of their mouth. They became careless with their speech and everything went downhill from there.

I've also seen big leaders who made millions of dollars in their Network Marketing businesses and today these businesses are still thriving after many years, because they still continue to do the things that caused their success. Even though they know everything about building their business, these leaders still read books and listen to CDs, because they know that if they stop, they will revert back to who they were before they achieved their success.

In the Network Marketing industry there is a common phrase, *"If you do what the successful people did, you too shall achieve great success."* There's also a second part that most people haven't heard... *"If you make the same mistakes that great leaders made, that caused their business empires to collapse, you too shall suffer the same fate."*

In the movie, 'Kingdom of Heaven,' Balian was being knighted by his father. He was to become the leader of his father's army. As he was on his knees, his father put a sword on his shoulder and began to knight him with the following oath: *"Be without fear in the face of your enemies. Be brave and upright, that God may love thee. Speak the truth always, even if it leads to your death. Safeguard the helpless and do no wrong. That is your oath!"* Then suddenly, with the back of his hand, the father struck Balian across his face and said, *"And that is so you remember it!"* Balian's father wanted him to never forget his oath, so he attached pain to it. You won't forget a lesson if you've suffered pain for it.

There are two types of leaders. Leaders who think short-term and leaders who think long-term. Short-term leaders only think about achieving their next goal regardless of how they do it. Long-term leaders think bigger. Not only do they think about achieving their next goal, but more importantly they think about how to sustain the success they aim to achieve as well as going beyond.

For the up and coming leaders, it is absolutely essential that they learn about the mistakes other great leaders in their field made that caused their businesses to fall so they can avoid the same fate. The only people that are qualified to teach us about those mistakes are the ones who have suffered the pain of those mistakes and survived. The pain will never let them forget the lessons they learned. The more we council and strategize with our respective leaders, the more we will learn about those great lessons; the mistakes that others made that we should avoid and never repeat.

Throughout the Bible, if you pay close attention, you will realize an amazing fact. The whole Bible is pointing out the mistakes that key people made in history. For thousands of years, every time a new leader appeared, the first role they had was to restore the mistakes of the past leader before they could move on to create new history. History will keep repeating itself until the mistake is fully restored.

Leadership in a Family

If you ask people, *"Who is the true leader of a family?"* most will say, *"The parents are the leaders, or the father is the leader, or in a single parent family, the mother is the leader."* This is a common mistake in family leadership. My belief is that the true leader of a family is neither the mother or the father. The 'active leaders' are the parents, but the *True Leader* of a family is the *Presence of God*... let me explain.

If God is removed from a family, the parents have literally taken the position of God and become a 'False God.' However, the parents are not perfect, so each and every time they make a mistake, their children witness their flaws and lose respect for them. Over many years of continuous mistakes, eventually the leadership of the parents will be in question or completely lost, causing the family unit to break down.

What is God?... God is Love. What is Love?... Love is a power. A power that unites two beings together. When God takes the rightful position as the True Leader of a family, the love of God unites all the members of the family and keeps the family together. When an individual has a personal relationship with God, it means they understand and know God's heart. When you are one with God's heart, you will know, because you will constantly be hearing in your heart and mind, words of love, respect, service, sacrifice and forgiveness. You will feel God encouraging and pushing you to: *"Forgive and love your parents anyway... Respect your father... Love your mother... Serve your parents... Look out for your brother and sister... Sacrifice!... Forgive!"*

Many confess to themselves, *"I do know God's Heart."*... But to know and not do, is to not know.

140

What is leadership?

According to John Maxwell, *"Leadership is influence."*... Therefore, when the presence God is the True Leader of a family, His love will *influence* each person in that family to act in a certain way towards one another. Removing God from a family is like removing the glue that keeps the family together. What is practiced within the family is then duplicated outside of it into the community and the world.

The Responsibility of a Leader

The number one responsibility of a leader is not to lead people, but to give them hope. Hope influences people to endure and keep fighting to achieve their dreams. The movie 'Jakob the Liar' is about a Jewish man named Jakob. Jakob and all the Jews in the area were being held captive by the Nazis in the ghettos of Poland during the Second World War. The Nazis prohibited all radio communication between the Jews and the outside world. They wanted to make sure the prisoners being held had no knowledge of how the war was going. They wanted to cripple the spirits of the Jews by removing their hope. Their strategy was that if they could steal their hope, they would be powerless to rise up against them. It did work and as a result, many Jews resorted to suicide, until this one day when Jakob heard a radio broadcast in a Nazi officer's barracks. The door was open and he heard the broadcaster say that the Russians were getting closer to Poland. Jakob knew that when the Russians got to Poland, the Jews would be freed. Immediately upon exiting the barracks, Jakob went and told a friend that the Russians were almost in Poland.

His friend asked him, *"How do you know this?... I heard it on the radio... You have a radio?... No! I heard the radio in the Nazi Barracks... No you didn't. You have a radio!... No, I don't have a radio... Of course you don't."*, his friend sarcastically remarked.

The next day Jakob found that his friend told some of the other people that he had a radio and that the Russians were getting closer to Poland. The rumor of Jakob having a radio spread throughout the ghettos. It lit up the people with hope. Those that were about to commit suicide suddenly changed their minds. They began to believe that it was only a matter of days before they would be free again.

A select group of men decided to create a resistance group so they could be ready to fight when the Russians arrived. They all pointed to Jakob to be their leader. It wasn't surprising since he was the only one giving them hope.

A few days later, the rumor of Jakob having a radio reached the Nazis. The Nazis tortured Jakob only to discover it was a lie. Jakob didn't have a radio, but the problem was that all the Jews still believed he did. The Nazis told Jakob they would execute him in front of all the people if he did not admit that there was no radio and that he was lying.

As Jakob stood on the platform with a gun to his head, he could see all the people desperately hanging on to the hope he had previously given them. He couldn't let them down. As a true leader, he refused to shatter their hopes. So at the sacrifice of his own life he falsely claimed, *"I have a radio!"*

This was truly a heartwarming example portraying the most important responsibility of leader... to give hope.

A few months before my father passed away, I remember receiving a testimonial from someone in India who had just finished reading my first book, *'How can I get myself to do what I need to do?'* The person said they were very inspired by my father's story of how he became successful in England when he couldn't even read or write English. The person commented that he must have been a great man. When I got this email I ran downstairs and read it to my father. I told him, *"See, people around the world who have never even met you think you're a great man!"* Tears of joy began to flow from his eyes. It's amazing how he was able to give hope to someone else on the other side of the world, who he didn't even know, by struggling and overcoming his own challenges.

Always keep in mind, as you stay determined and persist to overcome your challenges, you will give hope to many people to also do the same.

Chapter 24

Prepare for the Tough Times

"Struggle is nature's way of strengthening."
   - John Locke, TV Series 'Lost'

When we're going through personal challenges and life becomes a huge struggle, doesn't it sometimes feel like we are the only ones going through the tough times? That no one else in history who made it big has ever had the same challenges as we do? Even though intellectually we know we're not the only ones that have ever had these challenges, emotionally it feels like it's only happening to us, and if it's only happening to us, we must be doing something wrong; we must be on the wrong road to success. Maybe it's time to quit and do something else that doesn't have these struggles and that will be the sign from God that we are finally doing the right thing, because there are no struggles.

A few years ago, I started noticing a pattern of things that seem to always happen after I made the decision to achieve a new goal... First, I would get excited about a new dream that I wanted to accomplish. Then I would set goals and make my plan of how I was going to achieve it. Then I would pray and ask God, *"What do you think God, should I go for it? Do you think I can do it?"* After praying, many times I would feel God saying to me, *"Yes, you can do it. I'm behind you 100%!"* Then I would hear the angels singing, *"Hallelujah, hallelujah, hallelujah!!!"* I would get all pumped up, *"This is going to be easy, because God is with me."* Then I would make the decision to start my journey. *"That's it, I'm doing it!"*

As soon as I hit my first obstacle, it felt as if I started to descend into a valley of frustration that kept getting deeper and deeper. Every time I set a new goal, and hit my first obstacle, the same thing would happen. I would automatically enter this valley where I would experience the same feelings over and over again, no matter what goal I was trying to achieve. When I finally achieved my goal, it was as though I had somehow gotten out of the valley. I called this my **'Victory Valley.'** I realized that all I had to do was get through the valley and I would achieve my goal.

143

Because this happened to me so many times, I started writing down the things that were happening to me as I was going into and through my Victory Valley. I wrote these experiences down because I thought, if I know what's going to happen I can mentally prepare myself for the valley the next time I set a goal. I'm going to share with you a list of things that I personally experienced almost every time I set a new goal and started on my journey:

1. Negative thoughts would start coming into my head. I have no idea where they were coming from, but they became louder and more frequent: *"It's not going to work!... I'm doing the wrong thing!... I got too excited and didn't think it through enough!... It's too risky!... I'm wasting my time!... This might happen and that might happen!"*

2. A loss of concentration. All of sudden I couldn't focus for long periods of time. I couldn't think straight. I couldn't create or come up with new ideas. My mind was spinning like crazy and I couldn't stop it. I couldn't relax even for a moment while I was in this stage of the valley.

3. A loss of motivation. My energy began to get drained as I battled with the negative thoughts in my head all day long. The stress started to influence my behaviour. I began to get frustrated with my kids and my wife for little things that normally wouldn't bother me. I found myself not wanting to talk to anyone and becoming very quiet around the house. My dream was no longer inspiring me as much as it did before; it seemed like it was losing its power.

4. Sometimes when I prayed, I would feel a spiritual emptiness. I was finding it difficult to make an emotional connection with God as I did previously. I felt like he wasn't listening anymore. Sometimes it felt as though God had actually left and abandoned me, just when I needed him the most. I felt completely alone as I was chasing my dream. It made me question whether or not I should keep going... Is God trying to tell me to quit?... I didn't know.

After going through many Victory Valley experiences personally, I realized, the Victory Valley experience will appear almost every time a new goal is set, in any area of life: learning a new language, doing exams for college, training for a sport, building a business... the bigger the goal, the longer and deeper the Victory Valley experience will be.

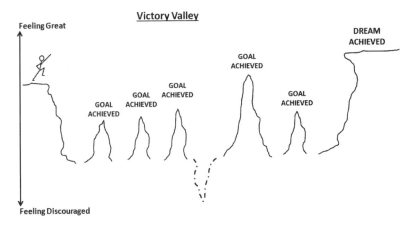

How do we endure and make it through Victory Valley successfully?
Your DREAM and your ATTITUDE will be your only guiding light out of Victory Valley.

YOUR DREAM

You have to continually ask yourself: *"Do I truly believe in my dream? Is my dream worth fighting for? Do I really want this? Do I really need this? If I accomplish my dream will it make me a better human being? Will it benefit my family? Will it allow me to make a positive difference in the world?"*

If your answer is *"Yes,"* you will keep going. The clearer your vision, the more power it will give you to endure through the valley. People quit not because the valley was too tough, but because their dream or vision was not clearly defined. They forgot why they started their journey and how they felt before they entered the valley.

Your dream better be burning in your heart, because when the crap hits you in the face it will be hard to see clearly.

YOUR ATTITUDE

1. We must understand why challenges come into our life. If we know why, we will be empowered to keep moving on.

Why Do Challenges Come Into My Life?

a. I created the challenge by my own mistake or stupidity.

b. God put the challenge in my way to protect me, change my direction or teach me something that I need to know for the future, so I must be grateful.

c. Someone else put that obstacle in my way for whatever reason and as long as I am true to God's values, God will take the pain that this obstacle has caused me and use it as a condition to bless my life in an *even greater* way than if the obstacle had never been put in my way, so I need to keep chasing my dream.

2. In order to achieve bigger goals in the future we need specific wisdom. This specific wisdom is only obtained by going through *certain* challenges that come into our lives. The challenge we are currently facing may actually be a key that opens the door to a higher level of success in the coming future, so stay strong and be determined to overcome it!

3. Sometimes, in order to achieve a higher level of success, the challenge we are confronting may be so tough that it will cause the *ground* below us to open up and cause us to fall to an even lower level of success than we currently have, before we can rise to an even higher level later on.

In the movie 'The Pursuit of Happyness,' when Chris Gardener decided to start his dream of being a stock broker, his financial situation and his personal life got even worse first, before it got better. As he trained for 6 months without receiving a paycheck: he ran out of money, couldn't pay his rent, his wife abandoned him and their son, he lost his home, he went from shelter to shelter with his young son and sometimes even had to sleep in a public washroom overnight. This was his Victory Valley on the way to becoming a qualified stock broker.

4. The pain in Victory Valley has a time limit. We only have to endure the pain for a certain period of time and then it will be over. Tough times don't last forever, they will always pass.

5. We need to borrow power from the life experiences of other people who have successfully made it through their Victory Valley, which was full of challenges even bigger than ours: business leaders and heroes throughout history... it's through their stories that we receive inspiration and hope. Hope is what empowers us to keep going through the challenges in our Victory Valley.

When great challenges come into our lives that are so tough and painful, they will push us to look for empowerment and peace in places we would never have thought of looking.

The movie 'Amistad' is a true story about a group of African men and women that were taken against their will from Africa to America to sell as slaves. They weren't just fighting for their freedom, they were fighting for their lives. They were taken to court by a number of different slave owners who were all claiming that they had the right to own them as their slaves. These Africans had witnessed rape, torture and murder of dozens of their fellow men & women along the journey to America. They knew that if they didn't win their freedom in court, they would be as good as dead. This was their Victory Valley. They suffered so much pain and were desperate for something they could believe in, anything that would give them even the slightest bit of hope.

One of the slaves, named of Yamba, was given a Bible by a protestor against slavery. He had no idea what the Bible was. He couldn't even read English. All he could do was to look at the pictures. For days he would stare at the pictures in the Bible trying to figure out what it was all about. *"Why was I given this book?"* On the very day that all hope seemed to be lost. The day they were predicted to lose the court battle and their lives, he figured out the story in the Bible. He turned to his friend, opened the Bible and began to explain what he felt the pictures on each page meant...

Yamba: *Look, their people have suffered more than ours. Their lives were full of suffering. Then he was born and everything changed.*

Joseph: *Who is he?*

Yamba: *I don't know, but everywhere he goes he is followed by the Sun. Here he is healing people with his hands, protecting them, being given children. He could also walk across the sea. But then something happened. He was captured. Accused of some sort of crime. Here he is with his hands tied.*

Joseph: *He must have done something!*

Yamba: *Why? What did we do?! Whatever it was, it was serious enough to kill him for it. Do you want to see how they killed him?*

Joseph: *This is just a story, Yamba!*

Yamba: *But look, that's not the end of it. His people took his body down from this thing... this... [He makes a sign of the cross in the air] They took him into a cave. They wrapped him in a cloth, like we do. They thought he was dead, but he appeared before his people again and spoke to them. Then finally, he rose into the sky. This is where the soul goes when you die. This is where we are going when they kill us. It doesn't look so bad. [he smiles]*

This is how Yamba made it through his Victory Valley. He held the Bible to his heart every time he went into the court room. However, his friend Joseph, wasn't ready to believe the message in the Bible. He got his strength and hope from a different source. When he was asked how he felt about the last fight in court, he said:

"We won't be going in alone! I will call into the past, to my ancestors, far back to the beginning of time and beg them to come and help me. I will reach back and draw them into me and they must come, for at this moment, I am the whole reason they have existed at all!"

6. Get mentally prepared for what is coming as you enter Victory Valley. In the movie, 'Rocky Balboa,' Rocky describes the Victory Valley brilliantly... *"The world ain't all sunshine and rainbows. It's a very mean and nasty place and I don't care how tough you are, it will beat you to your knees and keep you there permanently if you let it. You, me, or nobody is gonna hit as hard as life. But it ain't about how hard you're hit. It's about*

CHAPTER 24: PREPARE FOR THE TOUGH TIMES

how hard you can get hit and keep moving forward. How much you can take and keep moving forward. That's how winning is done!" Every time I set a new goal to accomplish something big in my life, I have a formula I follow that empowers me to successfully get through Victory Valley as quickly as possible. I tell myself...

"Terry, be prepared for what will come as soon as you set the goal and make the decision to start your journey. You're going to have negative thoughts enter your mind. Be ready for when they come!
Fight back and stay on track by reading positive books!

Next, you're going to experience times when you lose concentration, focus and creativity. Be ready for when it comes!
Be patient and keep working harder!

Next, you're going to experience a loss of motivation and energy. Sometimes your dream will seem powerless. Be ready for when that happens! It's only temporary, stay focussed. Work even harder!

Next, you're going to start to question whether or not your dream is worth the fight; should you quit or keep going? Be ready for when that happens!
This is normal, work even harder!

Next, your stress level is going to rise. You're going to get frustrated with your family members more easily. Be ready for when that happens!
Read positive books and keep your mind focussed!

Next, there are going to be times when you become quiet. You won't want to say anything, because you'll be feeling discouraged. You're going to be busy wrestling with your negative thoughts. Be ready for when that happens!
Keep reading, strengthen your mind. Watch those powerful movies!

Next, your prayers are going to seem empty. You're going to feel like you've lost your emotional connection with God. It's going to feel as though he's not listening anymore. Be ready for when that happens!
Pray harder anyway! He is listening, even if you don't feel it!

149

Next, you're going to feel as though God has abandoned you. You're going to feel totally alone on your journey. Be ready for when that happens! **Pray even harder and tell God, "I understand what's happening. I know you have to leave me temporarily in order for me to grow. It's okay, I can handle it. Even though it feels like you've abandoned me, I will not abandon you. I will not lose faith in you no matter what hardships I have to go through. I will keep working harder and harder to earn your respect. I know you will be back soon. Thank you for believing in me. I won't let you down!"**

It is very important to understand that the journey through Victory Valley can last weeks, months or sometimes even years depending on the size of your dream, so be prepared to keep up the fight for as long as it takes.

Mike Murdock, a Christian minister and speaker, refers to the Victory Valley as different seasons in our life. He says that what determines how long we stay in a season depends on our wisdom. The more correct knowledge we acquire and apply, the faster we will get out of the valley. You must constantly acquire knowledge from those who have travelled the journey before you, in order to shorten your time in the valley.

Like the seasons, when a new tough time enters our life, it will most likely look different than the previous one. If the tough times are always going to surprise us by the way they are dressed, how can we possibly prepare for them? We can only prepare for them mentally. Reading books on personal growth, attitude, character and spirituality, will make us mentally tougher and better prepared to emotionally handle whatever tough times enter our life. My spiritual mentor explains Victory Valley in this way:

"When a person enters Victory Valley, he has chosen to <u>suffer willingly</u> and pay the price in order to accomplish his goal. Suffering willingly is not suffering, it is creation... <u>creation of your future</u>."

Every time I got close to coming out of Victory Valley, all of a sudden I didn't feel alone anymore. My prayers became so much more empowering. I could feel that God was back. My connection with him became even more stronger because I didn't lose faith, because I didn't curse him for my suffering and because I didn't quit. When a person comes out of Victory Valley they are no longer the same person. Not only will they have achieved their current goal, but the struggles they went through will cause them to grow mentally, emotionally and spiritually.

For me personally, going through Victory Valley not only resulted in me achieving my goal, but more importantly it helped me develop a closer relationship with God. As I was going through the struggles, not only would I tell God about the pain I was feeling in my heart, but at the same time, I would tell him, *"It's okay, you don't have to worry about me. I'm going to make it. I won't let you down. I won't quit. I'm doing this for you!"*

Understanding Victory Valley changed my life and it can change yours too.

Chapter 25

Prepare for the Critic

*"The degree to which people say you are brainwashed,
is a measure of your conviction."*

- Rev Sun Myung Moon

If you do great things, you will receive great praise <u>AND</u> criticism. If you do nothing, you will receive no praise, but you will still receive criticism for doing nothing. It's a package deal. No matter what you do, criticism will always come in the package, so you might as well do what you want to do. Every time you act upon the advice of a critic with the intention of silencing him, your very action to do exactly that, will birth new critics that you didn't have before. So, like William Wallace's father says in the movie 'Braveheart,' *"Your heart is free, have the courage to follow it!"* You must ignore the naysayers. You must ignore what they think and say. They don't feel your pain! They don't have the hopes and dreams that you have for your life! Follow *your* heart!

When I wrote my first book, before I distributed a single copy, I wanted to prepare myself mentally for the critics and for what I knew was going to come sooner or later. I wrote this message to myself... *"Be ready for the critics. Some of your biggest critics will be people that you never expected; people who are in positions that could help you in a big way, but will choose not to. At the same time, be ready for those special people, that you never knew before or expected, who will come into your life and help you in ways you could never imagine."*

Even though it is extremely difficult, try and develop an attitude of gratitude for the critics. Be thankful for the critics. They will force you to refine yourself and become better and stronger. If you had no critics, you wouldn't change. You wouldn't push yourself to grow and become better. You don't have to agree with them, but learn to have empathy for your critics' viewpoints. If you had your critics' experiences, you would be saying the same thing. Respect the critic from their viewpoint, because from their point of view they are right. And from your viewpoint you are also right. So keep doing what you're doing if you truly have conviction for it. After preaching and getting a lot of rejection and criticism from people, Jesus' disciples came to him discouraged and looking for encouragement. Jesus told his disciples:

"He who has ears to hear, let him hear... And whosoever shall not receive you, nor hear your words, when ye depart out of that house or city, shake off the dust of your feet."

When you are showing your business plan to prospects, it is not your responsibility to push and hard sell the opportunity. Your responsibility is to simply do your very best at presenting the opportunity. Your prospect's responsibility however, is to _recognize_ it as the opportunity that could change their life... **all the pressure is on them!** If they fail to recognize it, they lose, and will suffer the consequences of a missed opportunity.

Never get angry at a prospect if they choose not to join your business, or a critic if they choose to criticize and persecute you. Always remember, you are 'THE DOOR' to everything great that has changed your life... When someone rejects your business or criticizes you, you must understand, it is only their opinion in the moment. Two, five or even ten years down the road, things in their life will change and so will their opinions. If you had shown them respect regardless of their viewpoint, when they are ready to make a change in their life they will surely connect with you and walk through *your* door. Some people may never have an interest in joining you in your business, but if they are impressed with the person you have become, they are sure to ask what has influenced you to become the person you are. Now you have the opportunity to share with them what is dear to your heart.

Whether you like it or not, knowingly or unknowingly, you are a representative. You represent everything that is important to you. You represent your business, you represent your faith, you represent your family and anything else you have great conviction in. The question is, what kind of representative are you? One that repels people because of your impatience and arrogance, or one that attracts people because of your kindness and respect?... The choice is yours.

Chapter 26

Power of Self Reflection

"Six mistakes mankind keeps making century after century:
Believing that personal gain is made by crushing others;
Worrying about things that cannot be changed or corrected;
Insisting that a thing is impossible because we cannot accomplish it;
Refusing to set aside trivial preferences;
Neglecting development and refinement of the mind;
Attempting to compel others to believe and live as we do."

- Cicero

A few years ago I remember being really frustrated with my level of success. I felt that I should have achieved so much more financially than I had. I was always working hard and felt it wasn't fair. When I prayed, I would plead with God: *"Why aren't you letting me be more successful?!*
I've worked so hard for so many years, I deserve to be more financially successful. It's not fair. How much more do I have to keep working and for how many more years? Why aren't you letting me have the financial success I deserve?"

I repeated this prayer many times. The answer I got back was the same every time: *"You're not ready yet. Your heart is not right. If you receive today the financial success you think you deserve, you will destroy your family and your life. You need to grow more. You need to develop your heart more. Become a better person and success will follow your growth."*

Looking back, if I had more financial success at that time, I would have divorced my wife. It would have been too easy to just leave when things got tough, rather than to try and change my stubborn, overpowering and impatient nature.

Why is it important to become a better person?

We see our challenges not as *they* are, but as *we* are. As we get better and stronger, the challenges that come into our life will appear smaller and easier to overcome.

Sir Edmund Hillary, who attempted to climb Mount Everest the first time and failed, looked at a picture of Mount Everest and said, *"Mount Everest, you have defeated me, but I will return and I will defeat you!... Because you can't get any bigger, but I can!"*

How do you become a better person?

People who read personal growth and spiritual books consistently, will automatically begin to pay attention to how they think, speak and act. The positive books they read will continually nudge and encourage them to change their behaviour towards becoming a more accepting, respectful, forgiving and loving person. People who don't read these kinds of books are usually oblivious to the way they behave and communicate with others. Motivation to change their behaviour usually only comes after the pain and suffering of numerous failed relationships.

If you want to improve a character trait, only a challenge in that area will cause you to become better. If you want to become stronger, you have no choice but to go through more challenges; you can't walk away when they come. If you want to develop more patience, you can only do that by going through situations of stress and frustration. If you want to become a more loving person, you need to start by loving the people who are tough to love in your own family.

One of the biggest life changers for me was when I decided to make an appointment with myself once a week. My goal was to design my ideal self and my ideal life; to really think about who I wanted to become, what I wanted to achieve and what I wanted to do with my life.

7 Pillars of a Great Life

1. Relationships
2. Faith
3. Health
4. Finances
5. Attitude *(How I See The World)*
6. Character *(How The World Sees Me, The Real Me)*
7. Dreams *(The World I Want To Create)*

1. Relationships

A few years ago, I was flipping the channels on TV and I came across a black and white movie that looked very interesting. I don't remember the title, but it showed a group of people sitting in a waiting room. They were all waiting for their name to be called out so they could enter through a set of big white doors. Some of them seemed pretty relaxed, while others were a little anxious about what was ahead of them. As each person entered the room, they were interviewed by a man in a white suit. As soon as I saw this man I thought to myself, *"I bet this movie is about the Spirit World. These people have all recently died and are waiting to see what happens to them. And the man in the white suit, he's got to be an angel."*

The camera began to focus on a nicely dressed old lady. She looked like she was a little disappointed having to sit next to the other people. They all looked a little below her status level. She had her fancy feather hat on and kept raising her nose as to avoid smelling the people close to her. She was trying to show her discontent for having to wait so long by sighing and fidgeting. Finally her turn came and she was asked to enter through the white doors.

When she went into the room, she was happy to see her late husband who had died a few years earlier, but her reaction to his presence was very reserved; as though she didn't really know how to fully express her love and joy. After she hugged him, she began to straighten out his tie and brush his shoulders, like she always did when they were alive. Her husband was also happy to see her, but suddenly he was reminded of how she always corrected him and made him feel.

The old lady then began to insist to the angel that she had a very beautiful house on earth, with a big garden and a yacht on the ocean. She demanded that she should have the same quality of life here, because she deserved it, after all the hard work she and her husband had done.

"Don't worry Madam, you will have everything that was important to you on earth," the Angel reassured the old lady. She smiled as though she won her demands.

A few moments later, the Angel announced that everything was ready and she could make her way to her residence. *"Please go through the red carpeted corridor and you will be shown to your beautiful home."*

The old lady got up and proceeded to direct her husband, *"Let's go!"* The Angel interrupted her and said, *"Oh, he can't go with you. You will only have the things that were important to you on earth: your house, your garden, your yacht, your clothes, your furniture, your jewellery. Only the things you valued will be accompanying you. No people. Just yourself. Alone... just the way you chose it be, when you were alive on earth."*

Only at that very moment did the old lady realize that the happiness she felt actually came from the relationships and not from all the things she was accumulating. Always keep in mind, the joy you feel in your life is actually coming to you from the relationships you have and not from the things you've achieved. If there was no one to witness your achievements, you would feel no lasting joy... it would all be for nothing.

Pay attention to the relationships around you as you live your life and pursue your dreams. If you have a good relationship with your spouse, with your children, with your co-workers and with your business associates, these relationships will only empower you to achieve greater success in everything you do.

If you achieve financial success while neglecting your family and hurting people along the way, your business may grow and become big for a while, but eventually it will fall. It's a law of the universe. Besides, what good is all the money if you have to live amongst broken relationships? There'll be no joy. Whatever happens in your personal life at home will always ultimately affect your performance in your professional life.

In the movie 'Great Debaters,' there is a scene where a 14 year old boy is being questioned by his father about his homework. The boy is standing in his father's office with his head bowed down in absolute fear. Behind the father were a library of books on display and at that very moment I thought to myself, *"What good are all the books you've read, if you can't even love your son in a way that he actually feels loved."*

Just because you are reading personal growth books, it does not mean your behaviour is going to change automatically. You must spend time in self-reflection and ask yourself regularly:

"Am I actually changing?... How can I improve?... What am I doing wrong?... What am I not doing?"

How can I be a better...

Husband or Wife? - What does your spouse continually complain about?
Father or Mother? - What do your children complain about?
Son or Daughter? - What do your parents complain about?
Brother or Sister? - What do your siblings complain about?
Leader, Co-Worker, Teammate? - What do your peers complain about?

I have often given blank cards or sent an email to my sons and my wife, asking them to help me become a better father and husband by telling me one or two things, at the most, that I can improve on in their eyes. I always tell them in jest, *"No more than two things. Let's not get carried away. I don't want my self-esteem completely destroyed."* It is probably more truth than jest.

This is not an easy thing to do especially if you can't face the truth, but if you truly want to become a better person and develop better relationships, this will get you straight to the very thing you need to focus on... the truth. And only they know what it really is.

On a blank card, I write each thing that I need to improve on. I call this my 'reminder card.' On the opposite side I write the same thing in a positive affirmation, as though I have already corrected it. This is what I read to myself on a regular basis, to remind me of how I should act.

I knew some of these things were going to take a long time to improve; they had become deeply ingrained habits of bad behaviour. I was determined to work on them for as long as it took, because I knew the consequences of not changing them would be far worse.

2. My Faith

A few years ago my older son said to me, *"Dad, I don't think I need God."* I'm sure he was waiting for an immediate strong comeback, but he didn't get one. Instead, I said something he never expected to hear. *"I agree! What do you need God for when you have parents? If you need anything you're going to ask us, not God."* He was surprised at my answer and thought I was finished. I wasn't quite finished yet... *"You might think that you don't need God today, because you have your parents, but one day in the future we're not going to be here. Never forget this! Everyone, with no exception, sooner or later, will get knocked down to their knees by different challenges that come into their life. When that happens to you, who are you going to turn to that you can truly trust? Don't wait until that day comes before you get to know Him. If you take time to search Him out and get to know His heart, He'll help you to avoid a lot of those challenges that are headed your way. God doesn't work on the outside like your parents, he works on the inside; in your heart and in your mind. Once you get to know Him personally, once you get to know His heart and how much He loves you, you'll have a tremendous sense of peace, power and wisdom that you can't get from anywhere or anyone in the universe. All you have to do is to reach out and just talk to Him, He'll do the rest."*

3. My Health

What do I need to be doing that I'm not doing?
Write a reminder card for each thing.

More often than not, achieving our goals and dreams take a lot longer than we expect. We must look after our health as we are chasing our passion. Don't create a problem for yourself that shows up when you finally achieve success.

Some people believe that God has chosen them to do something great with their lives through their passion. If this is true for you, than I am sure he is also depending on you to look after your health so you can successfully carry out that mission!

4. My Finances

To increase my income in my job or business, what do I need to be doing that I'm not doing enough of?
Write a reminder card for each thing.

5. Attitude (How I see the world)

How is my attitude?... Do I complain a lot?... Do I bring energy into a room or do I drain the energy with my negativity?... Do I repel or attract people?... How do I react to things that don't go my way?... How is my language?... What am I saying or doing that I know is not good?

If you really want the truth, be brave and ask someone!
Write a reminder card for each thing.

6. My Character (How the world sees me, the real me)

It's easy to fake your character outside your home because it's only for a short time. Our real character or real self is the person we are when we are at home; when we are with our family, and even more so, when we are alone. When we don't have to impress anyone, are we still kind, caring, respectful, and thoughtful? Do we still go out of our way to help each other? Do we still talk to each other nicely? Do we still say, please and thank you?

I remember a time when I was invited to a friend's get-together. This one person brought their little kids over. One of the kids was misbehaving and broke something on the table. The mother of the child started getting angry at her son and instantly the man who owned the house said, in a gentle sweet voice, *"Don't get angry, he's only a child."* He then picked up the boy and comforted him. He looked like a model father to everyone who didn't know him personally. I was pleasantly surprised and at the same time absolutely disgusted with him. I was so angry inside because I knew how poorly this man treated his own children. This display of behaviour was not his true character.

On this particular day a few years ago. I was stressed about some things in my life and I had just lost my temper with one of my sons. I was sitting in the living room and as I glanced up at the wall in front of me and saw dozens of personal growth books on the bookshelf, I instantly heard a voice in my head, *"Anyone can be kind and caring when things are going great and they're feeling good."* At that moment I realized, the true character of a person is revealed by the way he treats others, when he himself is under pressure and not feeling his best.

If I had a visitor in my house, I never would have lost my temper with my son so easily. No way! I would have been on my best behaviour, because I would not want to damage my reputation. So why was I behaving this way with my son when there were no visitors? It's because I thought there was nothing to lose. As I thought more about it, I realized, there is a great deal to lose! Even more than my reputation. By losing my temper so easily, I can emotionally hurt my son and if I keep doing it, I will lose my son. My relationship with my son is more important than impressing a visitor. From that day on, I realized that my true character is revealed by the way I treat my wife and kids in my home, when no one else is there to witness.

7. My Dreams (The world I want to create)

What is your passion?
What is your purpose in life?
What do you want to become?
When you have the answers to these questions, your life will move to a whole new level. Write them down.

Every time I read my reminder cards, my behaviour in some areas of my life changed instantly for a certain period of time. Not permanently. Sometimes it was only for one hour. Yet even if it was only for one hour, it was still an improvement! The more times you read your reminder cards the more your behaviour will start to change for longer periods of time.

I realized that when my wife and kids are out and I know that they will be home soon, it's a good time to quickly read my reminder cards just before they get home. If we claim to love our family more than anyone else in the world, then we should treat them that way.

The only real proof of whether or not we have truly changed for the better, comes from our own family and the people we work with. It doesn't matter what *we* think, if we want to know the truth, we need to ask our spouse, our children, and our peers whether or not we have changed and become better. That's the real proof.

Are you brave enough to ask?

Chapter 27

Power of God's Love

"One word frees us of all the weight and pain of life,
that word is love."

- Sophodes

When I was 14 years old my father purchased a retail property across the street from where we lived. He knew I had an interest in business and said to me, *"I want you to manage the store. Think about what you would like to sell in it and we'll go and get the merchandise. We can hire an employee to look after the store during the day and then you can take over once you come home from school."*

I told my father, *"I think we should sell sportswear."* He didn't even hesitate and said, *"Okay, go ahead and contact the suppliers."* I picked up the phone and called my number one choice first, Adidas. The receptionist told me that we had to go to their sports exhibition to see the merchandise and set up an account. When we got to the exhibition, I did all the talking with the sales rep myself, my father didn't say a word, *his presence* alone, gave me all the confidence I needed. The sales rep told me that the Adidas company had a policy for setting up new accounts. The first order had to be a minimum of £2000, at the time that was almost $4000. When I told my father, he simply said, *"Okay."* I put the order together with the help of the sales rep and then my father pulled out his cheque book.

Over the next few weeks we went to numerous other suppliers and purchased more inventory. My father probably spent close to $8000 in the initial inventory and never questioned any of my decisions or showed that he was worried about any mistakes I could possibly make. I never understood or appreciated what my father actually did for me then, until after he died, 30 years later. Only as I looked back as an adult, after he was gone, could I see how much my father really believed in me. How much faith he had in me. How much he really trusted me. He risked so much of his money on my dream and on my ability to make the right decision. I was a 14-year-old boy and he went completely along with whatever decision I made. It took 30 years and losing my father, before realizing the greatness of his actions. In the movie 'Immortals,' Zeus, the God of all Gods was speaking to Theseus, a human being who was greatly struggling and lacking belief in himself. With tears in his eyes, Zeus said to him, *"No God will ever again come to your aid. You are on your own, do you understand, mortal?... I have faith in you Theseus, prove me right!.... Lead your people!"*

When I heard these words in this movie, it reminded me of what my dad did for me: By risking all that money on a 14-year-old boy, he was saying to me by his actions, *"I have faith in you, prove me right!"*

Sometimes when we ask God to help us through our struggles and we feel that he isn't helping us, he is actually helping us by not helping us the way we want him to. He is showing us that he has faith in us and that we can solve the problem at hand without him. As we solve our problems, our self-esteem increases. The success of solving the problem at hand increases our confidence in order to solve bigger problems that lie ahead.

I always used to wonder, how does God actually help a person? As I was searching for this answer in different spiritual books, I found out that God helps people similar to the way parents help their children. When our parents took us to school on the very first day, they didn't come in and sit at our desk and do our work for us. They left us at school after reassuring us, *"You'll be okay!"* Inside us, we had a belief that came from our parents that we would be okay. Because we trusted our parents completely, we believed what they said. When we truly know that someone believes in us, someone that we trust completely, that belief lives inside of us. It's a feeling that we can connect with, whenever we need the power to do something uncomfortable.

In the same way, the more we pray and learn about God's heart, the more we learn to trust and have faith in Him. As our relationship becomes stronger and stronger, we advance to where we can actually feel God's presence, His love deep inside our heart. When we connect with it, it will empower us to overcome painful challenges and do great things with our lives.

How does God's love comfort us?

We hear many people confess that God's love has given them so much peace. How does a person receive God's love? How does God heal and remove the pain in their heart?

All we have to do is ask God to come into our heart and be a part of our lives. He will never refuse us. Our free will has kept Him at the door-step of our life eagerly awaiting an invitation. Just like a parent waiting for his child to open up and ask for help, God, our Heavenly Parent is desperately waiting for his children to reach out to Him as well.

A few years ago at 1:00am in the morning, I was suddenly awoken by the ringing of the phone. When I put it to my ear, I heard the horrific screams of a young girl. I can still hear them as if it was yesterday, *"Something's happened to my mom! Something's happened to my mom!"* The call was from my 11-year-old niece. Her mother had just committed suicide. The cause was found to be severe depression. Many family members tried to comfort the father, but how could they possibly succeed in comforting him when they themselves had never experienced *his* pain?

As a part of the healing process the father was encouraged to go to counseling. His counselor was a lady who had experienced the exact same thing. Her husband had also committed suicide many years earlier. The father told me that she was the one who made the most difference in his healing process. She was the only one who knew exactly how he felt. She had already cried the tears he was crying and truly understood his pain.

I learned from a spiritual mentor of mine, *"Only the person who has cried more tears than you, can truly comfort you."*

Where does God live?...Where does he want to live?... If you were a child, where would you want to live?... With your parents, right? So, it makes sense to believe that God would also want to live in the heart and mind of his children. As God lives in the heart of his children, he experiences everything his children experience. Every joy and every bit of sorrow that his children feel, he too feels it to his core, but a thousand times more intensely. One of the greatest stories that affected my life in a big way, was about a woman who experienced the presence of God through a spiritual experience in her dream. All her life she believed God to be this powerful mighty being with no feelings, sitting on a throne, judging human beings after their lives had ended. He would be the one deciding who goes to heaven and who goes to hell. And if and when he sent them to hell, he would do it without any remorse.

This woman said that in her dream she was taken up to the Spirit World to meet God. Suddenly she entered an area of extreme light. It was brighter than the sun, but not painful. It was extremely beautiful. She felt like she was wrapped in a blanket of love, as though God was holding her like a baby. She felt completely surrounded and protected by love. She had never felt such an incredibly warm & wonderful feeling. She felt completely loved and joy filled.

All of a sudden a grey cloud appeared. As she slowly entered the cloud, she began to feel an enormous amount of sadness. When she went deeper into the cloud she began to feel more and more sorrow. Tears began to fall down her cheeks. She couldn't stop crying. Her heart felt like it was going to burst with sadness. There was so much sorrow surrounding her. She asked her guide, *"Where am I?... There is so much sadness here. My heart is breaking and I don't know why."* All of a sudden she realized exactly where she was. She was in God's heart. She could feel God's pain and sorrow. His tears were flowing like a waterfall. She could feel everything God was feeling. She reached out and asked God, *"Heavenly Father why are you so sad?"* She could feel his reply in her heart.

"My child, if you could see the world through My eyes what would you see? How would you feel? Your own children abusing and killing each other. Treating each other worse than animals. Endless suffering, conflict and wars. My child, I don't just see it, I feel it in the hearts of my children. Every tear they cry, I cry a thousand. Every bit of pain and sorrow they experience, I feel my heart being torn into pieces. I can feel everything that my children feel. I am trying to rescue them. Oh, if they would only listen to their hearts."

Suddenly she awoke. Her pillow was completely soaked in tears. From that day on, she vowed to stop God's tears and ease the pain & sorrow in His heart. She vowed to tell people about God's broken heart and how he truly loves his children.

The following is a conversation between Paul Edgecomb (prison warden) and John Coffey (prisoner and miracle man/angel), from the movie 'Green Mile:'

Paul Edgecomb:

On the day of my judgment, when I stand before God, and He asks me why did I kill one of his true miracles, what am I gonna say? That it was my job?... My job?!"

John Coffey:

You tell God the Father, it was a kindness you done. I know you're hurtin' and worryin.' I can feel it on you, but you oughta quit on it now because I want it over and done. I do. I'm tired boss. Tired of bein' on the road, lonely as a sparrow in the rain. Tired of not ever having me a buddy to be with, to tell me where we's coming from or going to, or why. Mostly I'm tired of people being ugly to each other. I'm tired of all the pain I feel and hear in the world every day. There's too much of it. It's like pieces of glass in my head all the time."

If God's messengers can feel the pain in the hearts of God's children, how much more pain does God feel?... So going back to the question, how does God's love comfort us?... Here's the answer: Because God *has cried more tears* and felt more pain than any one of his children, as we ask Him to come into our hearts, His love will comfort us and heal our wounds by removing the pain in our hearts... as His love enters our heart it pushes out the pain.

When Jesus was asked, *"Which is the greatest commandment?"* He replied: *"Thou shalt love the Lord thy God with all thy heart, and with all thy soul, and with all thy mind. This is the first and great commandment. And the second is like unto it, Thou shalt love thy neighbour as thyself. On these two commandments hang all the law and the prophets.*" Jesus was telling the people to love God, because he clearly knew that God's heart was broken. If you truly love God with all your heart, you will begin to sense how He feels. If you know that God's heart is broken, you will want to reach out and comfort Him. By loving our neighbours, God's children, God is comforted. The very desire to comfort God will automatically heal the wounds and remove the pain in our own heart.

There are 2 types of people:

People who need God to comfort them, and those who want to comfort God by connecting with His heart through prayer and doing His Will to make this world a better place.

Which one are you?

Chapter 28

Power of Inner Peace

*"Forgiveness is the fragrance that the violet sheds
on the heel that crushed it."*

- Mark Twain

For many years, one of the most frustrating things I wrestled with as I tried to manage my events of the day, was that when I focused all my energy on chasing my dreams, all of a sudden I would feel tremendous guilt for neglecting my family, or my health, or my spiritual life. The guilt would literally cause me to stop building my business and change my direction. After a little while, I would then feel guilty that my business was going to suffer if I didn't give it enough effort, so I went back in the other direction. Back and forth like a pendulum, one way then the other. It was driving me crazy! The guilt was killing my energy. I had to figure out a way to get rid of it. After trying many different things, here's what finally worked and gave me the peace I was looking for:

1 - Prayer
Prayer is the first priority of my day, whether it is for 2 minutes or 20 minutes, it is the number one priority of my day. Here's why... the day I die will most likely be totally unexpected to myself and my family. I want to make sure I'm ready for that day, whenever it is. I don't want any regrets. If God decides that today is that day, I'm ready. The only thing that will give me the peace to accept this inevitable fact is my relationship with my Heavenly Father. I have no regrets and look forward to that day with peace and joy in my heart, whenever it is,

2 - Family
I ask each member of my family, *"Is there anything I can do for you?"* It is my responsibility as the 'active' leader of my family, to look after their needs! It takes less than 5 minutes to ask. Once I know what they need, I can then set aside the time to do it whenever it needs to be done, but now I have the peace to get on with my day.

3 - Health

I make sure that I have set aside time to exercise. Whenever that is, it is fixed in my schedule. If I am not healthy and fit I cannot chase my dreams, I cannot look after my family and God will not be able to use me to make a difference in the world. It is my responsibility to God, my family and myself to keep my body healthy and fit. When I know that I have set aside the time to exercise it gives me the peace to get on with my day.

Now, knowing that I have taken care of my relationship with God, my family and my health, I am ready! Ready to chase my passion! The inner peace I have, which has replaced the guilt, will now empower me to chase my passion with even more determination and power.

Forgiveness

There is one step remaining to gaining total inner peace. Even if a person carries out the three things mentioned above, total inner peace will still elude them if they hold resentment against another human being. As you pray with sincerity, you cannot possibly expect God to forgive you for your mistakes if you hold resentment or hatred towards another. Your prayers will not give you peace. You must forgive the person you have resentment towards before you can experience complete inner peace. Forgiveness will give you inner peace! Many people say, *"I forgive, but I won't forget."* This is not true forgiveness. To forgive, *is* to forget! It is extremely difficult and very painful, but it is the only way to truly forgive another.

In the 1961 movie 'A Raisin in the Sun' there is a truly beautiful and moving example of a mother's forgiveness. After receiving some life insurance money for the death of her husband, the mother gives her son a large part of it to put in the bank. The son however, disobeys her. Instead, he takes the money and loses it in an investment scam. When the mother finds out, here's what she says:

"Your father came in night after night with the red showing in his eyes and the veins showing in his head. I saw him grow old and thin before he was 40. Working and working, like somebody's old horse. Killing himself... and you went and lost everything he worked for his whole life!"

169

Her heart was torn to pieces. She felt so betrayed by the son she so dearly loved. The following day, the mother had a conversation with her daughter after she heard her cursing her brother:

"He's not a man, he's nothing but a toothless rat. He's no brother of mine!"
"I thought I taught you to love him."
"Love him?... There's nothing left to love."
"There's always something left to love. Have you cried for that boy today? I don't mean for yourself and for the family because we lost the money. I mean for him and what he's gone through. And God help him! God help him, what it's done to him. Child, when do you think is the time to love somebody the most? When he's done good and made things easy for everybody?... No! No, that ain't the time at all. It's when he's at his lowest and he can't believe in himself because the world's done whipped him so. When you start measuring somebody, measure them right child, measure them right. You make sure that you take into account the hills and the valleys he's come through to get to wherever he is."

This mother exemplifies true forgiveness. She chose to forgive, forget and to continue to love her son in the midst of her pain. It's easy to forgive and forget when you're not hurting, but it takes a big heart to forgive when you're still in pain.

In the movie 'Les Miserables' starring Liam Neeson, there is another exceptional example of forgiveness in the midst of pain:

A priest welcomed a homeless thief into his house. He gave him food and a bed to sleep on. During the night, the thief decided to steal whatever he could. As he was in the process, the priest awoke and startled the thief. The thief panicked, and then punched the priest in the face and ran off with the silverware. The next day, the thief is brought back in chains to the priest's home by the police. They told the priest that the thief had said, *"The priest gave me the silverware."* They didn't believe him and wanted to get a confirmation from the priest himself. The priest, with fresh bruises on his face said, *"I did give him the silverware. I even told him to take the silver candlesticks but he didn't."* Then he asked his assistant to fetch the candle sticks and put them in the thief's bag. The thief was absolutely astounded.

When the police left, the thief asked the priest, *"Why did you do what you did?... Why did you save me?"* The priest replied, *"You no longer belong to evil. With this silver, I bought your soul. I've ransomed you from fear and hatred, now I give you back to God."*

This was a true man of God. He chose to forgive, forget and continue to love in the midst of his pain. What a beautiful example of forgiveness

Chapter 29

Conclusion

"Tell me what you pay attention to and I will tell you who you are."

- José Ortega y Gasset

Financial Freedom vs. True Freedom

Many years ago when my older son was about 6-years-old, he asked me two profound questions: *"Why should I be good?"* ... *"Why can't I just do what I want to do?"* He caught me completely off guard. I was shocked to hear these questions, especially from a 6-year-old. I reacted and gave him a quick answer that satisfied him enough to not ask me anymore questions. However, I knew it was not the best answer. After he left the room, I became very curious to search out a better answer for myself. As I diligently went through my spiritual books, I discovered the following truth:

"The greater the love you show on earth to humanity and creation, the greater the freedom you will have in the Spirit World, for you will be welcomed everywhere."

People talk about financial freedom all the time. *"The more money you have, the more freedom you'll have."* I agree with this statement fully. However, the more I deliberated over this statement and compared it with the statement I found in my spiritual books, I came to the conclusion that financial freedom still does not give you True Freedom.

Financial Freedom comes to those who earn an ongoing income. An ongoing or residual income gives you the freedom to chase your passion, because you have the money and the time.

True Freedom comes only to those who have an ongoing income AND a great reputation. These people are free to go wherever they want to go, for they are welcomed everywhere.

172

A great reputation takes years to build, so we need to start early and most importantly, we need to be aware of what can harm or kill our reputation. If we know what that is, we will stay away from it.

Develop A Sense of Urgency

It is very important to accept the fact that we have a limited amount of time to accomplish our dreams and purpose in life. It is not about how long we are going to live, but about how many productive years we have left. We may live to be a hundred, but it would be sad if the last 10 to 15 years were lived in a bed. So many people assume they have all the time in the world and waste years of their productive life by not doing what they need to do with a sense of urgency.

People who do things with a sense of urgency get things done. Imagine if you accepted the fact that all you had left was 10 more years. 10 more years to accomplish all your desires in life. That's it!!! Now you have a deadline.

Now, how would you plan your life?
Now, how would you live?
Now, how seriously would you treat each day?
Now, how much you would accomplish?

If you need to get some great things accomplished in a short period of time and you are *very serious* and *ready to do whatever it takes*, this prayer may helpful:

"Dear Heavenly Father, please help me do in the next 2 years, what would normally take 20."

A Person of Great Value

Don't strive only to achieve success, but as Albert Einstein said, *"Strive to become a person of great value."* In the movie 'Meet Joe Black,' Bill Parish was a man who had achieved the ultimate level of success in modern society. He attained tremendous financial wealth, a beautiful family and a great reputation. His daughter even said to him, *"Dad, everyone who ever meets you, loves you."* A few weeks prior to his 65th birthday, the Angel of Death came to visit Bill. The Angel told Bill that even though he had come to take him, he would like to make a deal with him. The Angel said to Bill...

"I have never seen a person like you before. I am impressed with the way you have lived your life. I would like to stay a while. Show me around in exchange for more time."

On the night of his 65th birthday after the celebrations, the Angel told Bill that his time was finally up. Bill looked over at the Angel and nervously asked, *"Should I be afraid?"*

The Angel replied, *"No. Not a man like you."*

I hope and wish upon you personally, that one day in the very distant future, when you get to ask the same question, *"Should I be afraid?"*... that you hear the same beautiful words in your heart...

"No, not a man like you." ... *"No, not a woman like you."*

"You did it right! You lived your life right."

A Message From The Author

My congratulations to you for finishing the book. I would love to hear from you in regards to how this book has helped you in your personal journey towards accomplishing your goals. I'm sure your story will inspire all who read it. I look forward to your email.

God Bless,

Terry Gogna

Terry Gogna
terry@terrygogna.com